THE CHILDREN'S FRONT

The Impact of the Second World War on
British Children

*A policeman looks on while a little evacuee takes a snack at a
London railway station.*

THE CHILDREN'S FRONT

The Impact of the Second World War on British Children

HENRY BUCKTON

PHILLIMORE

2009

Published by
PHILLIMORE & CO. LTD
Chichester, West Sussex, England

www.phillimore.co.uk
www.thehistorypress.co.uk

ISBN 978-1-86077-571-0

Printed and bound in Great Britain

Contents

List of Illustrations

Acknowledgements

I would like to thank the following for help with memories, photographs and other information: Mrs K. Aitchison, Deanna Allan, Doreen Ayling, John Ayling, Julie Baker, Margaret Ball, Gerald Bartlett, Vena Bartlett, Elizabeth Berens, Diana Bewers, Anne Biffin, Colin Bishop, Rosa Bowler, Jean Bradley, Margaret Cable, Alan Cairns, Ken Carruthers, Joyce Caskey, Peter Cattermole, Arthur William Henry Charles, Paul Chryst, Don Cook, Mary Cooper, Dion Copley, Shirley Copley, Joyce Copper, Sylvia Cowcill, Jack Davie, Philip Everest, Gladys Fellingham, Betty Field, Ethel Fisher, Betty Fletcher, Doreen Foreman, Pamela Gear, Allan George, Elizabeth Gillett, Maureen Goffin, Doreen Govan, Geoff Grater, Ron Green, Joyce Hallewell, Gerald Hamer, Jean Hamer, Margaret Harber, Bill Hawkins, Ted Hedges, Frank Hind, John Hoggard, Andrew Howat, Betty Howat, Bill Johnson, Nova Jones, Bruce Kean, Alan Kerry, Tony King, Molly Kinghorn, Moya Knight, Gerald Lettice, Mrs V. J. Lewis, Cyril Licquorish, Joy Matthews, Pamela Moyse, Betty Parkyn, Donald Patience, Jenny Peacock, Jean Pearse, Norman Pirie, Sheila Pitman, Gerald Poole, Audrey Purser, Barbara Raine, Donald Raine, Hazel Reigate, June Richards, Peter Richards, Johnny Ringwood, Pat Robinson, Colin Russell, Pamela Scott, Doreen Shephard, Frank Stanford, Roy Stevens, Winifred Margaret Taylor, Margaret Thipthorpe, Allan Thomas, Iris Thomas, Mike Thomas, Bill Underwood, June Van Dam, Jacqueline Watson, Colin Webb, Gerald Webb, Jean Wells, Margaret Wilce, Doreen Wilde, Myra Williams, Barbara Wood and Marilyn Wood.

Thanks to Duncan Lucas, for allowing me to use information contained in, and quote from, his book *One Man's Wigston*, published by Sutton Publishing: copyright O.D. Lucas. Thanks also to Mr Lucas for supplying material from the Greater Wigston Historical Society and obtaining permission to use information contained in and quote from: J.R. Colver's paper on the Government Evacuation Scheme and Doreen Boulter's booklet entitled *Wiggy's War*. Thanks to Marie Litchfield, for allowing me to quote from her book *Countryside & Cloister*, published by Family Publications: copyright Family Publications. Thanks also to Family Publications for their permission. Thanks to William Moore, for allowing me to use information contained in, and quote from his book, *Hard Times and Humour*. Thanks to Joe Crowfoot for permission to reproduce his paintings (www.joecrowfootartist.co.uk). Thanks to Harry and Edna Dickinson of Home Front Friends. Thanks also for the photographs of Bisley School, reproduced by permission of Surrey History Centre.

I would also like to thank Dame Eileen Atkins DBE, Sir Chris Bonington CBE, Raymond Briggs, Geoffrey Burgon, Bruce Forsyth CBE, Frederick Forsyth, Lord Hurd of Westwell CH, CBE, PC, Malcolm Laycock, Miriam Margolyes, Colin Skipp, and Michael Winner, whose stories in this book are reproduced from articles originally written for a series of booklets in aid of the BBC Children In Need Appeal, compiled and published by Henry Buckton, and are reproduced with their permission: *Celebrity Snapshots*, *Celebrity Childhood Memories*, *Celebrity Child's Play* and *Celebrity School Days*.

Many of the photographs have been reproduced from *Hutchinson's Pictorial History of the War*. The drawings, maps and photographs were largely commissioned by Walter Hutchinson, and Virtue and Company Limited, during the progress of the war, and made a unique record of events. They are reproduced with the kind permission of Michael Virtue, Virtue Books Limited, Grindfield Farm, Furners Green, Uckfield, East Sussex.

Introduction

Some of our most vivid and poignant memories stem from our childhood. This is particularly true for people who were children in Britain during the Second World War. Their recollections are enhanced by an extraordinary succession of events and circumstances, that burned lasting imagery into their minds. They had a childhood unlike any other generation throughout history. In this book, through both historical research and the memories of those who were children at the time, many of the major factors that impacted on children's lives are examined. There are stories written by people from very different backgrounds and areas of Britain who shared the common bond of being children during this unique period.

At a time when children were in mortal danger because of daily attacks on British soil, the book looks at the measures taken to protect them, such as gas masks, air-raid shelters and the black-out. The land, became an island fortress as the paraphernalia of war in the form of military installations and equipment appeared everywhere, from cities to quiet rural villages. Also discussed are the effects of having fathers and other members of the family away from home, serving in the armed forces. The importance of play at this time is reflected in the toys they would have known, the games they enjoyed, the ways they were entertained and informed, and the clubs they could join. Some describe 'doing their bit' for the war effort, while others talk about their experience of evacuation, feelings ranging from happiness and security, to fear and abuse.

Finally, there is an insight into the turbulent emotional roller-coaster ride for children during wartime, horrors experienced during nightmare attacks on London and other cities, contrasting with the exuberant relief of final victory and the homecoming of loved ones.

Chapter 1

Transition from Peace to War

In the late 1930s any astute child must have been aware that war was on the cards, even if they were not aware of or interested in the political situation in Europe. But up and down the land, in homes ranging from the affluent to the impoverished, things were changing. An unprecedented gloom underpinned the conversations of the adult members of households. There was tension and anxiety as people talked endlessly about political figures, the rise of Adolf Hitler, and the last war, which had ended only twenty years earlier but had cost the lives of an estimated 888,000 British men and 1.8 million of Germany's male population. From city suburbs to quiet country lanes, everyone was united in solemn expectation.

The Summer of 1939

In the final few weeks before the declaration of war, at the beginning of September 1939, while adults debated the rocky road ahead, school children were enjoying their summer holiday. From Bristol, ten-year-old Doreen Govan, along with her mother, father and grandparents, was heading for a fortnight at Goodrington in South Devon. They had been there the year before and, having enjoyed it, had decided to return, this time including the extravagance of hiring a beach hut.

When at last the great day arrived, Doreen was brimming with excitement at the prospect of boarding 'the great chuffing train' at Stapleton Road station, and the subsequent rail journey with changes at Temple Meads and Exeter St David's. The trunk with the necessary clothes and accoutrements had preceded them on an earlier train to await their arrival.

Doreen explains that in those days people dressed up more, and wearing good clothes for travelling was essential as it created a good impression. During the working week her father wore a suit, while for holidays he donned a pair of grey flannel trousers and a tweed sports jacket. Her mother, accustomed to being smartly dressed, sported a navy blue outfit complete with matching hat and gloves and, of course, stockings and court shoes. Her grandfather was dressed in similar style to her father, while her practically minded grandmother was attired more appropriately for the season with a light summer dress, cardigan and straw hat. However, and much to her annoyance, Doreen had been forced into wearing her best winter dress, made of russet-coloured wool with long sleeves. The only explanation for this she can offer, is that all her summer clothes had been packed away for the journey. To complete the ensemble, she wore her 'much-hated Panama hat, white ankle socks and black patent ankle strap shoes'.

1   *Doreen Govan explains that, even while on holiday, people dressed up more in the 1930s and 1940s: 'It created a good impression.' Here a 14-year-old Pat Robinson, on the right, enjoys a break to Weston-super-Mare around 1942, which shows that some families still managed to get away, despite the war.*

The family had taken digs in Paignton but on arrival at the railway station struggled directly to their beach hut at Goodrington, up one side of a hill and down the other, in order to deposit their deck-chairs. Grandfather marched on ahead with his wife some distance behind him, while Doreen and her parents, with a deck-chair apiece, straggled in an angry little knot even further behind. Doreen admits to grizzling as only an 'overdressed, uncomfortable ten-year-old girl can grizzle'.

After this inauspicious start the rest of the fortnight was 'idyllic'. Could a major war really have been so close? Every day the beach teemed with families from different parts of the country. There was laughter and joy as children played ball games, built sandcastles, and spent more time in the sea than out of it. Doreen's father paid the lifeguard sixpence a day to teach his daughter to swim; and he did, quite successfully.

Doreen made particular friends with a pair of twins from another beach hut, a boy and girl from London who she describes as looking very exotic with dark skins and curly black hair. Their mother was white and she overheard her own mother and grandmother describing them in undertones as 'half-caste', a term new to her. Some of the parents would not allow their children to play with the twins and Doreen could not understand why. Fortunately there were plenty of others who, like herself, sought their company. In retrospect, she considers this to have been her first awareness of racial prejudice.

It seems that even here tension simmered beneath the surface. For instance, in the hut next to Doreen's family were two young married couples. The two husbands and one of the wives took great pleasure in joining the children at play, especially during their group ball games. The second wife, obviously not interested, always sat by herself. Doreen's father labelled her 'a miserable bitch', but perhaps there was more to it than met the eye? One of the young men was a pilot in the RAF, who often discussed the possibility of war. He was confident that war was imminent and that he would be among the first 'to go'. Doreen remembers the consternation this caused her own father.

2 *Seaside holidays to English resorts were very popular with British children in the 1930s, although largely, they would soon become a thing of the past. In this photograph taken just before the war, Pat Robinson and her brother are enjoying a typical summer holiday in Weston-super-Mare.*

'Meanwhile,' she expands, 'time passed in a heady haze of sunshine, sea and sand, with the pleasures of ice-creams, lemonade and candyfloss on hand. Tea was brewed in the hut, in a kettle on a little spirit stove. To this day the smell of meths always evokes the memory of that holiday.' All of these things must have seemed quite normal to British children, but within a very short period, ice-cream would be unobtainable and forgotten, and tea was strictly rationed.

'All too soon,' Doreen concludes, 'the two weeks were up and it was back home on the train to Bristol.' This would prove to be her last such holiday for many a year. When they did get back to the city, the news everywhere was that war seemed a certainty. The authorities in Bristol appeared to be making frantic preparations, in case the worst should happen.

In the north of England, at the mining village of Great Clifton in Cumbria, Ken Carruthers experienced a break of a different sort and admits that his first realisation that anything was actually kicking off was on the day before war was declared. He attended Chapel Brow School where, at the end of the summer term, pupils had been asked to submit their names if they wished to attend a fortnight's holiday at Drigg near Whitehaven. This free vacation was aimed at the less healthy among the children and was organised by the local school authorities. Being of sound health, Ken put his name forward but did not expect for one moment to be chosen. As it turned out he was, and he can only assume that it was to make up the numbers.

They arrived at the camp at Drigg one week before war was declared and any notion of a holiday in the sunshine was quickly dispelled when they were thrown together with the children from other participating villages for extra lessons. It was like being back at school. However, on the first Saturday after arriving, which was 2 September 1939, they were given immediate notice to prepare to go home again. By noon a fleet of buses had arrived to take them back to their respective villages, thus ending their break one week prematurely.

Ken's parents knew nothing of this until he arrived back on their doorstep. They automatically assumed he had been sent home early for doing something wrong, 'for, believe me,' he admits, 'trouble was my middle name and I was blamed for all sorts of misdemeanours, mostly things of which I knew nothing'.

3   *Beach boy Douglas Hurd on the left enjoying a day at the seaside with friends. Born in 1930, the ex-Foreign Secretary recalls his wartime childhood, including what happened in the Wiltshire village of Oare in 1940, when everyone believed the Germans had invaded.*

So the summer holiday of 1939 drew to its close as children returned home to a world in suspense. Adults had known for some time that a continental war was almost unavoidable. Everywhere preparations for conflict were being hurriedly put in place, while politicians endeavoured to reach a last minute peaceful solution.

The Day of Declaration

A particular moment that has stuck in the mind of most people who were children at the time was the declaration of war itself. At 11.15am on Sunday 3 September 1939, Neville Chamberlain announced to a hushed nation that we were at war with Germany. Most memories relate to entire families waiting for this broadcast to be made on the wireless, in order to hear for themselves the final outcome of the government's diplomacy and political bargaining.

At Great Clifton, the father of Ken Carruthers had bought the family's very first wireless especially for the occasion. Following the announcement, most of the women in the village rushed out of their homes to console each other, many in tears, the tragedies of the First World War still fresh in their family annals. Many of them had lost fathers, sons or husbands during that conflict. A little while later the school learned that the reason the children had been rushed home from their holiday in Drigg was to prepare the camp for expected evacuees.

Fresh from her holiday in Devon, Doreen Govan was aware of the desperate measures taking effect, but 3 September seemed like any other Sunday. The roast was in the oven, her father had peeled the vegetables, and a rice pudding simmered on the bottom shelf. However, the household did seem unusually subdued.

Doreen was in the garden when her father summoned her back into the house, insisting that she hear a speech about to be broadcast on the wireless. Her mother was sitting in her armchair looking very worried. Serious music filled the air and the sombre tones of the Prime Minister finally relayed the news that people had been dreading.

Deep in rural Somerset, in the village of Ashcott, some five miles from Glastonbury and three from Street, Marie Litchfield lived with her mother, father, sister Antoinette, nicknamed 'Bou', and brother Simon; there was another baby on the way, Bridget, who was born on 9 October 1939. Marie's father had lost the use of one arm at the battle of Passchendaele during the First World War. The previous night there had been high winds resulting in a few tiles being blown off the roof of their house. Two young brothers who lived down the road came with a ladder to fix them back on, and afterwards they were invited to come into the living-room to listen to the announcement with the rest of her family, as they did not have the luxury of a wireless at their own home.

In 1939 many households did not have a radio. At Axmouth in South Devon, June Richards was six years old when her entire family descended on her

4   *Doreen Govan is pictured in 1939, front row far right, with other children from Eastville Junior Mixed School, Bristol. Many are carrying their gas masks. Some boxes are still attached to their original string, while others have a variety of home-made straps.*

5   *An indication of what was to come. Two hundred young German Jews, the first of many thousand refugees, arrive in Harwich in February 1938.*

grandmother's house next door to listen to the announcement. She recalls how the Prime Minister's announcement 'that no such undertaking has been received' caused both her mother and grandmother to cry, and she could not understand why. 'Surely,' she innocently thought, 'some one could make sure that an undertaking could be received,' especially if it stopped people crying and being unhappy.

In Devizes in Wiltshire, Bill Underwood lived with his family in rooms attached to the rear of his father's barber's shop in Sheep Street. At the time there was no electricity in the house, so lighting was provided by gas and heating by a small coal fire. All cooking was done in the coal cellar where a gas stove had been installed. At the beginning of the war his family consisted of mum, dad and eight children. One of his brothers slept at an auntie's house and one of his sisters slept at their grandmother's home. It might have been a Sunday, and a day of some magnitude, but with such a large family to support life had to go on, so Bill's father spent the day visiting sick and elderly customers, who were unable to come into the shop during the week. However, the remainder of his family were waiting by the wireless, and although the adults seemed deflated by the news Bill recalls how the children, especially in the street and later at school, greeted it with euphoria.

Barbara Raine associates the day of declaration with chickens. Just before the war began her father's annual leave from the Bradford Police Force was cancelled due to the political situation. Her mother decided to take her to stay with a married cousin in Norfolk. At the bottom of their back garden was a chicken run and it was one of Barbara's morning duties to take any food scraps from the breakfast table to mix with their feed. On the day in question she discovered that one 'weak little chick', was struggling to get to its feet and being trampled on by the others. Somewhat distressed she ran back into the house to report the situation. 'Uncle Henry, Uncle Henry,' she cried, just as Chamberlain's speech was about to commence. All the adults in the room greeted her with 'Shush, be quiet! Sit down and stop talking.' Barbara had never been told off like this before and, not understanding what she had done wrong, burst into tears! Later, she was hugged and kissed and in her words 'made better'.

Many people recall that shortly after the Prime Minister's speech had finished the air-raid sirens sounded, sending them scuttling for cover. As the decision to sound these alarms was taken locally, this could have been for several reasons, but they were all of course false alarms. However, the person responsible for sounding the siren in Brighton at 10am, which was one hour before the speech, remembered by nine-year-old Elizabeth Gillett, must surely have been suffering from an attack of the jitters.

As well as the famous speech by Neville Chamberlain, the King also broadcast a message to the nation that day. It marked a turning point in the lives of millions of people, and for children throughout Britain things would never be the same again.

6   *Early in the war the King and Queen visit India House in London, where the little daughter of the Deputy High Commissioner presents the Queen with a bouquet of flowers.*

The Twilight War

Following the declaration of war there was a period when little seemed to happen militarily but, because of the way their peers and elders had been talking, a lot of children expected the Nazis to drop in at any moment. This period of military inactivity became known as the 'Phoney War', which is generally accepted as being the period between September 1939 and April 1940. The term was first used, allegedly, by an American senator called William Edgar Borah, who died in January 1940. However, in September 1939 he claimed: 'Lord, if I could only have talked to Hitler, all of this might have been avoided.' Winston Churchill referred to the same period as the 'Twilight War', while the British press dubbed it 'Sitzkrieg', or the 'sitting war'.

Although little seemed to happen between the warring armies, at home it was a time when attitudes were understandably changing as tension mounted. Marie Litchfield's mother was a music teacher and her daughters had acquired a passionate love for the works of the great German composers, such as Beethoven and Mozart, and come to admire all things German, including their current emblems. Marie explains that:

> One of the first things Bou and I had to do was to take down all the iron crosses and swastikas we had crayoned on large pieces of paper and hung up in the windows. For us there was nothing political intended. Germany was the home of many of our beloved composers, so we were mad about anything German. It was all right before the hostilities began; but Father had to point out to us very seriously that he, or we, might be arrested and put into prison if we didn't take them down TODAY. We did so, but reluctantly – children hate being told that they have got to do something, and normally our parents were very good at not making this mistake.

Frank Hind, who was born in 1936, lived in the rented wing of an old farmhouse at Cheddon Fitzpaine, some two miles from Taunton. For some time an elderly German Jew, a refugee from Nazi oppression, had been living in a little bungalow in the parish, 'an inoffensive professional type'. One night his windows were smashed and 'HUN OUT!' scrawled on his walls. 'Dad put it down to ignorance,' Frank explains, 'disgraceful but understandable in view of all the anti-German propaganda and feeling at that time'.

Winifred Margaret Taylor (née Austin), who was 12 years old when war was declared, lived in an area of the London docks called Custom House, adjacent to the Royal Docks. She has clear memories of an Italian café near her home where she occasionally enjoyed lemon ice. 'I can see it now,' she reflects, 'it was snow white with pieces of lemon.' After Italy declared war on Britain on 10 June 1940, a mob descended on the café and the owners were taken away in a police van, presumably for their own safety, although many Italian nationals were interred at this time, in case they posed an internal security threat. However, the 'old chap' who ran the business was evidently released, as some time later he was observed sitting in the road, dirty, distressed and talking to himself.

In Leeds, where eight-year-old Molly Kinghorn lived, the Phoney War brought an end to her and her sister's social aspirations. They had been getting very excited, having just attended final fittings for the bridesmaids' dresses they were due to wear in September at the wedding of their cousin Tommy from Doncaster. According to Molly, the pink satin garments were truly lovely, 'all shiny and silky'. Then, to their utter dismay, war was declared and it was decreed that no travel was allowed unless absolutely necessary. So their long awaited bridesmaid duties were subsequently cancelled.

In Wigston, now a suburb of Leicester, Doreen Boulter noted that places of entertainment such as theatres and dance halls were closed down as soon as hostilities were announced. 'Mind you,' she writes, 'after a short time they all reopened again, when it was discovered we were not all going to be blown to bits at once.' Her mother had been instructing her in the art of ballroom dancing at Wigston's Co-op Hall, where they enjoyed what are now referred to as 'old time dances'. In fact, Doreen danced the Lambeth Walk all around The Marine at Great Yarmouth on her last holiday before the war. 'I thought the band would never stop,' she explains. 'We went right round the balcony. Great stuff!'

Doreen was never allowed to stay to the very end of these dances as her mother considered them far too late. So towards the end of the evening the young girl changed

7 *Belgian children and their mothers welcome troops of the British Expeditionary Force as they pass through town on their way to the front.*

8   *At the start of the war thousands of continental families came to Britain to escape from the advancing Nazis, including this Belgian mother and her children, who have arrived at Victoria station.*

into woollen stockings and lace-up shoes for the journey home. Then, clutching her sequined bag and silver shoes, the couple would depart as the band always seemed to be playing 'I'll See you in my Dreams'. Doreen states that, for some reason she could never fathom, her mother did not approve of quicksteps or tangos.

In May 1940 the Phoney War came to an abrupt end. After the declaration of war, the British Expeditionary Force was sent to France to help bolster the French defences against a German invasion. By May 1940 the Germans had assembled a vast army along their western borders, consisting of over two and a half million men. On 10 May, and with lightning speed, the German army launched the Blitzkreig. The two armies appeared quite balanced on paper, although the Allies had considerably more tanks than their enemy. when the fighting began the huge French army, of mainly conscripted and poorly trained soldiers, put up little resistance and the tiny British element was forced back to the sea, where they were evacuated from the beaches of Dunkirk.

Back in Britain, children knew nothing of what was occurring on the continent, believing the British army to be invincible. So when word got around Bristol that they were bringing the soldiers home, Doreen Govan explains that kids were confused. They could only assume that the soldiers would be coming home victorious, so when it was announced that the army would be arriving at Stapleton Road station, women and children in their droves went down to cheer them. Those who still had Union Jacks or favours left over from the coronation of King George and Queen Elizabeth took them to wave. There was great excitement, but the sight that met their eyes was not what they had expected, as Doreen explains:

I shall never forget what we saw that day. Train after train was pulling in and unloading soldiers from the carriages. The men were dirty, unshaven and desperately tired: most of the uniforms were tattered. Some soldiers were being helped along between two comrades, some were on crutches, others wearing dirty blood-stained bandages. Word got round that there were French and Belgian soldiers among them. How we cheered those soldiers as they were transferred into buses to be taken to their next destination, which turned out to be Eastville Park. Despite the battle fatigue the soldiers smiled and waved back and some of them threw foreign coins out to the children below. We heard later that the soldiers were bewildered at the enthusiastic welcome home. 'After all, we were defeated' they were alleged to have said. The buses took them off to Eastville Park, which had been hastily commandeered but not barbed-wired. What seemed like hundreds of khaki army tents had been put up in neat rows and the soldiers were posted there for the wounded to be treated and to be given rest before being sent back to their regiments to go where they were needed next.

9   *Several children are among this group of Dutch refugees lining up at Liverpool Street Station. These were the lucky ones. Soon it would be almost impossible to escape from the occupied countries of Europe.*

As an army reservist, the father of Mrs V.J. Lewis, who lived in Coventry, had been called up straight away. He had worked at the Courtaulds factory that had begun to make silk for parachutes. After he left, his wife was offered a job there in his place: 'I suppose the management looked after army wives,' thinks Mrs Lewis. Her father proceeded to France with the BEF, after which they heard very little from him, except a brief card to say he was well. Then, one morning at about 2am, pebbles were thrown at her mother's window. Her husband was standing outside the house. He explained that he had escaped from the beaches of Dunkirk on a boat and after arriving in England had come directly home to let his wife know that he was OK. He stayed a while and then disappeared back into the darkness, as he attempted to get back to his regiment. By the time his daughter awoke in the morning, he had already gone. She was terribly disappointed to have missed him, but fortunately he survived the war and left the army to be reunited with his family sometime before D-Day.

Chapter 2

Preparing for the Worst

From the outset of war school children faced a changed regime, now including things like what to do in an air raid and how to put on the dreaded gas mask, with its horrible rubbery smell. They also learned about air raid precautions and how to cope in the black-out. Lesson practice soon turned to reality, and as the war progressed the valuable skills they learned at this time helped save many young lives.

Issue of Gas Masks

The issue of a gas mask to every person in the country, either directly before or shortly after the declaration of war, was one of a series of measures that make us realise the government expected hostilities were almost a foregone conclusion. By 1940, 38 million gas masks had been issued, an undertaking and expense that would not have been entered into lightly. During the First World War the Germans had used deadly mustard gas against soldiers in the trenches, so the use of similar agents against civilian targets, delivered by bombs dropped from aircraft, was considered a distinct probability.

Teenagers and older children were issued with the standard adult mask. These were made of black rubber and had a single perspex eye-strip. Younger children were issued with a mask that the authorities cunningly named a 'Mickey Mouse', in order to encourage them to be worn. They were made of red rubber, had blue canisters and two separate eye-pieces with bright rims. They made the wearer look nothing like Mickey Mouse, nor were they any fun to put on! Both masks were fitted with canisters containing charcoal that could soak up any poison. Depending on where you lived, there were different arrangements for the issue of masks.

In Devizes, Bill Underwood had to go to the schoolrooms in Sheep Street. He was fitted with an adult mask but recalls that his youngest sister Mary was issued with the Mickey Mouse variety. At the village of Avoch on Highland's Black Isle, Donald Patience, issued with an adult mask, was quite perturbed at having the single strip of perspex to see through 'instead of two separate eyes'. Deanna Allan who lived at Corby in Northamptonshire notes, 'We kids had to practise putting on our Mickey Mouse gas masks, the smell of the rubber and the claustrophobic feeling making us shed many a tear.' Deanna admits that her mother was a bit soft hearted, and did not try to force the issue, so it was just as well she never had to use the mask for real.

In Bristol, after arriving home from school one day, Doreen Govan was informed that, along with her mother, grandmother, and all other women and children in the area, she was to go immediately to the local police station to be fitted

10 *Look, it's Mickey Mouse! A young Rosa Bowler wearing her gas mask.*

with her mask. All the local men were instructed to report after 6pm, when they had finished work. Doreen notes:

> In those days police stations were not in the least intimidating, with open doors and a large wooden counter. They were staffed by big burly men, who were always friendly to children and ever ready to accept a found purse (sometimes with a reward if you were lucky) or hear details about a strayed pet. I knew many of the children from my area and it was almost a fun day to us in the excitement of a new experience. Not so for the women. My Gran was terrified of the forthcoming war and everything that it would mean: after all she was a soldier's daughter and had lived through two wars already, the Boer War and the First World War.

After some time it was Doreen's turn to be fitted, and although she was only ten years old she was old enough for the adult mask. It was made of heavy black rubber and had straps that went round the back of her head. Any difficulty with breathing while wearing it, would cause the perspex eye-piece to steam up. Doreen's mother could only manage to keep hers on for around thirty seconds before she began to gag for air and whipped it off. Her grandmother simply turned completely white. Neither of them thought they would be able to wear it for any length of time, should there ever be a gas attack.

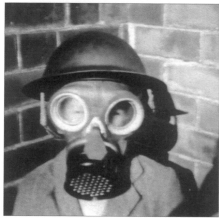

11 *John Hoggard wearing his gas mask and older brother's steel helmet.*

Each gas mask was issued in a wooden box attached to a piece of string, which children were expected to carry everywhere with them. If they arrived at school without it for instance, they could be sent home to fetch it. Mothers often decorated the boxes to make them a little more appealing, or gave them colourful straps. Some children used them to carry their sandwiches to school, or they became receptacles for things like sweets, hair slides and other small objects.

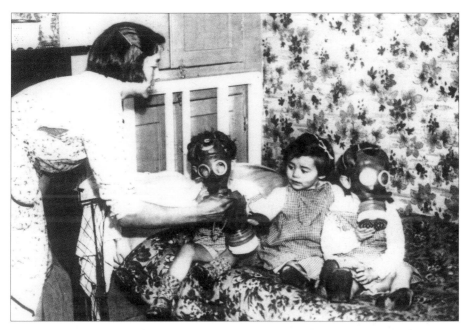

12 *Brighton triplets, Leslie, Joyce and John Ferris, are pictured here putting on their gas masks, with a little help from mum.*

Ethel Fisher recalls that at Flimby Girls School near the town of Maryport in Cumbria they were subjected to a weekly practice, which was announced by a teacher ringing the school bell at an unexpected time. Every scholar had to stop whatever they were doing, and immediately put on their mask. These were worn for approximately ten minutes before being removed, allowing lessons to be resumed. Several people describe how during such practices they 'grunted' at each other, pretending to be pigs.

There was a third type of mask specifically for babies, which was more of a helmet in which the infant was totally enveloped. Air could be pumped into it by means of a bellows. At Axmouth, when June Richards made her way to the schoolroom to be fitted with her mask, she remembers being quite excited, until she saw the 'thing' her baby brother was destined to use. She describes how the baby was placed completely inside it, which was then sealed by the pulling of a drawstring. 'Someone had to keep pumping a bellows-like device to keep the air going through the mask,' she explains. 'I hated it! Nevertheless we all had to take turns with the pump.' At Ashcott, where baby Bridget was born in October, Marie Litchfield was equally distressed by the 'terrifying box in which

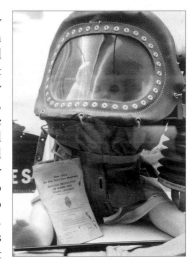

13 *Example of a gas mask issued to mothers with babies.*

mothers had to put the baby and pump with filtered air'. Her mother could hardly bear to look at it. The whole lot, she explains, masks and their boxes, were packed away in a cupboard near the front door where they were out of sight yet near at hand if needed.

The government took the issue of wearing gas masks very seriously indeed. ARP wardens were instructed to carry out monthly inspections of them. If you were caught without your mask you could be fined, and if you lost it you would be forced to pay for a replacement. Chemists were recruited by the government and formed into local Gas Identification Squads, and the tops of pillar boxes were painted with a special gas detector agent. Leaflets were distributed among the public telling them how to identify the different poisons the enemy might use.

With the government's hard line stance on the wearing of gas masks, some people began to take the issue equally seriously, especially after the first German air raids began over Britain. The first attack on mainland Britain was directed against ships of the Royal Navy anchored at Rosyth in the Firth of Forth on 16 October 1939, but before long German aircraft were becoming frequent visitors in the sky, particularly over southern England. The county of Kent was Britain's front line, so when there was a gas attack warning at St Margaret's at Cliffe, near Dover, in November 1939, young Frank Stanford and his mother donned their masks immediately. The warning of a gas attack would be issued by an ARP warden giving blasts on a whistle and sounding a rattle, the sort used by football supporters. At about 8pm, while Frank and his mother were listening to the wireless, they became aware of the local ARP warden in the street issuing his warning:

> We put our gas masks on. They were not the nicest of things to wear but we sat waiting for the all clear. This would be only blasts on the whistle, but no rattle. After an hour our cat came into the room and sat in front of the fire. Mother wondered why it wasn't suffering ill effects from the gas. After a lengthy period still waiting for the all clear, my brother who was on leave from the Royal Navy arrived home from a visit to the pictures with his girl friend. What a shock for them to see us sitting with our gas masks on. Of course it was a false alarm and the ARP man had forgotten to do his rounds to give us the all clear.

After many months had passed, and other areas had suffered false alarms from over-zealous ARP officers, people became complacent about gas attacks. More often than not the box was left under the stairs when they went out and the Germans never did use poison gas on Britain during the Second World War.

Air raid Precautions

The ARP warden was a figure who would become very familiar to children through-out the country, as the issuer of various warnings. His main purpose was to warn people against the threat of bombing.

For Molly Kinghorn in Leeds the ARP man was particularly familiar because he was her father. Being 44 years of age and too old for active service he became an ARP warden for his area of the city. He wore a black helmet emblazoned with a large white W. His house was marked with the letters SP to indicate that it stored a stirrup pump and a bucket of water. He also had buckets of sand, which together with the water could be used to help extinguish nearby fires. Similarly, the father of six-year-old Margaret Wilce was an ARP warden for the village of Walford near Ross-on-Wye. When the siren sounded in Ross, he would put on his ARP suit and helmet, and together with other local wardens commence his patrol. He was responsible for the distribution and fitting of gas masks in a certain part of Walford. Margaret often went with him along the lanes and footpaths to the outlying cottages. He had to inspect the masks from time to time, and later in the war had to attach a green filter to them, when it was feared a different gas could be used in attacks. 'Luckily we never had to use them,' she confirms, 'but I remember taking mine to school in its box which had a rexine cover made by my mother.'

Air-raid sirens themselves were often mounted on public buildings, including schools. Doreen Govan describes their warning sound as a 'gut-curdling undulating wail' which would send you scuttling to the shelter, where you would remain until the relief of the all clear, which was a long, continuous blast.

Of course not everywhere had the luxury of an air-raid siren. In the rural village of Huggate in the Yorkshire Wolds, where John Hoggard's father was a special constable and his brother was an ARP warden, they had no telephone at home but lived next door to the full-time village bobby and had access to his. As there were no sirens, when their neighbour received telephone warning of a possible air attack, he would pass it on to John's brother who, with his ARP helmet on, would cycle around the village blowing blasts on a whistle. This is similar to the gas attack warning mentioned earlier, but without the rattle. The all clear involved another round of the village, this time expelling a more sustained blow.

Some ARP wardens were constantly on alert; others hardly knew there was a war on. Arthur William Henry Charles, lived on a farm half way between the Pembrokeshire villages of Porthgain and Llanrhian, which he says was in a 'fairly safe part of Wales'. The village experienced only one air-raid warning during the whole of the war. Because of the novelty of the incident, Mr Charles recalls it well. The local warden was the miller and, having

14 *Maureen Goffin is seen here using ARP sand, kept in a bin to put out fires, to make sand pies on the steps of the house where she lived in Wallasey. The wrought iron gates were later collected for the war effort.*

15   Rosa Bowler looks on from the safety of the doorway as her family practises putting out a fire with a stirrup pump. Her grandfather is on the pump and her mother nearest the water butt, while her aunt fetches the water. The lady on the hose is Miss Parry, a London school teacher who lodged with them at the time.

received the alert, he departed with great urgency on his bicycle blowing frantically on his whistle 'till he was nearly out of breath'. The school children were dispatched to the cemetery, where they took shelter behind the tombstones. 'The headmaster probably presumed that the Germans would not bother bombing the dead.' By the time the miller returned from his rounds the all clear had come through, but he was too exhausted to make the return trip. 'So we are still waiting for the all clear,' concludes Mr Charles, although he admits that the children are no longer waiting in the cemetery.

But what would happen in an air raid to deaf people? Betty Fletcher's parents were both profoundly deaf and dumb, although she, an only child, had hearing. When the air-raid warnings began at night, her father installed a wire going up the wall of the house, which led through the bedroom window and was fixed to the corner of his pillow. When the siren sounded, a neighbour would pull hard on the other end of the wire and the pillow would shoot out from under her father's head. Betty would then be quickly woken and taken down to the shelter. Born in 1937, Betty soon learnt to get herself up when the siren went off. She would run into her parents' room, shake her mother awake and using sign language say 'Guns! Guns!' Then they would all hurry to the shelter in the garden.

Doreen Govan relates that on the Sunday war was declared, the church bells were sounded for the last time. The War Office had decreed that the ringing of church bells was to be the national warning signal in the event of an aerial attack by German parachutists. Ex-Foreign Secretary Douglas Hurd explains that in his village the church bells were also used to announce the presence of enemy troops in their midst. He recounts that:

> One morning during the summer holidays of 1940 news reached us in the small Wiltshire village of Oare that the German invasion had begun. I remember being puzzled that the church bells had not rung as we had been told would happen. Nevertheless I sat up in bed, aged ten, clasping a rather heavy silver-coloured revolver, ready to do my bit. The revolver fired caps, but they were loud enough to frighten our Nanny, and I thought that they might have a good effect on the Wehrmacht. Fortunately for this theory, the rumour proved false.

While they were at school, children would have to rely on their teachers but if they were caught in the open after an air attack had begun, they would have to be responsible for their own safety. The following are the air raid instructions issued to staff and pupils at Eye Area School in Suffolk, but no doubt similar instructions were circulated elsewhere.

- There is as much danger from shrapnel fire from anti-aircraft guns and from bullets fired from aircraft fighting overhead as there is from bombs. You MUST NOT therefore on any account stand in the open looking up at the sky.

- If actual bombing finds you in the street take cover in the nearest doorway, entrance, or opening and lie flat. If you cannot keep all your body under cover at least keep your head under cover. Place your coat (folded), or any book you have with you, on your head.

- Never lie down in the road if you can get on to some soft ground. Splinters will rebound from the road.

- If you hear bombs exploding put a pencil, a stick, a piece of rubber or a cork between your teeth to keep your mouth open. This will help to avoid injury to your ears by concussion from explosions.

- Please study the above very carefully, do not destroy it, but keep it by you to refresh your memory from time to time.

Air-raid shelters

Wherever you were, if the warning of air attack was sounded, you were expected to take cover. For this purpose air-raid shelters were provided. In 1938 Sir John Anderson took charge of the ARP and commissioned an engineer called William Patterson to design a personal shelter that could protect families in their gardens. These shelters became known as Anderson shelters, and over the next few years two

million were distributed to British households in areas considered likely to be bombed.

Anderson shelters were designed to accommodate six people. They were made of curved sheets of corrugated iron, bolted together at the top. Each end had a steel plate, and some people included an earthen blast wall. Once constructed, they were half-buried in the ground and then covered with earth to add extra protection. They were issued free of charge unless your father earned more than £5 a week, in which case he had to purchase it for £7.

Doreen Govan recalls the Anderson shelter that was delivered to their garden in Bristol. It came with a bag of nuts and bolts and 'scant instructions as to how to erect it'. She describes how a three-foot hole was dug into which the shelter was lowered. The displaced earth was then piled on top, and for some 'unaccountable reason' her mother grew marrows on the roof.

At first people would go down to their air-raid shelters at night whether the sirens had gone or not. Doreen found it to be 'cold, miserable and damp in a hole in the ground at night', and describes how the condensation ran down the corrugated iron

16   *Drawing made by the artist Bill Ward in 1939, of the construction of an Anderson shelter.*

and made all their bedding wet. The only heat came from a paraffin stove and the lighting was provided by small oil lamps. Doreen and her mother shared their shelter with Mrs Upton from next door and her daughter Sheila. Her husband was serving with the Royal Navy in the Indian Ocean and they didn't see him for five years.

Many houses in the area had a poster up in the front window with a large black S on a white background. This signified that anyone, particularly children, unlucky enough to be caught out when the sirens sounded was welcome to take refuge in the householder's shelter. At Corby, Deanna Allan notes how her grandmother installed every home comfort in her Anderson shelter, even stopping to fill hot water bottles after the air-raid siren had gone 'rather defeating the object!' she says and explains that the only problem blighting this 'bomb-proof des-res' was the constant flooding. In the Elephant and Castle district of London, Mike Thomas writes that after the beginning of the Blitz, their cat always seemed to

17   *Delivery of Anderson shelters to the public somewhere in London,*
25 February 1939.

know when an air raid was imminent, even before the warning sounded. It would get into the Anderson shelter ahead of the family, thus providing them with their very own early warning system.

Some people simply could not afford £7 to buy a shelter for their gardens, so DIY became a popular way of protecting your family. At the village of Ash near Martock in Somerset, the father of Shirley Copley took the building of his family shelter very seriously as they were close to the aircraft factories at Yeovil. He dug a hole in the back lawn, but as this kept filling up with water something more substantial was obviously required. At the back of the house was a high bank covered with bushes, so he dug into this to produce a shelter, which he then lined with planks of wood. The young Shirley loved it, turning his effort into a Wendy house and decorating the edges of the planks with bits of broken china she found in the garden.

The first communal shelters, in 1938, were the requisitioned basements and cellars of many properties. Also, trenches were dug in the parks of large towns and cities. During the Blitz these trenches were lined and covered with concrete or steel. Able to hold around fifty people, they were wet, uncomfortable and unpopular. In March 1940 the government began to build more substantial community shelters, also designed to protect around fifty people. These were made of brick and concrete

18   *The first communal shelters were the requisitioned basements and cellars of many properties. Londoners queue up outside a block of offices with mattresses and cushions, ready to sleep in the basement for the night.*

and surrounded with sandbags, so they provided more protection than Anderson shelters. However, within months the building of these came to a virtual standstill because of a severe shortage of cement. Doreen Govan notes that in Bristol most streets were allocated one of these shelters. However, the public perception was that they were no safer than their own homes so they didn't bother using them. And, anyway, after the creation of the Local Defence Volunteers in May 1940 the shelters were often occupied by their number while on fire-watching or other duties. Another problem with public shelters, as explained by Ken Carruthers at Great Clifton, was that people started to use them as toilets on their way home from the pub, so they were deemed useless for the purpose intended.

During the Blitz the people of London took refuge in tube stations. They would buy platform tickets for a penny-halfpenny and then camp on the platforms for the night. These were popular because they were dry, warm and quiet. But tube stations were not as safe as people thought. High explosive bombs dropped by the Luftwaffe could penetrate up to fifty feet through solid ground. The worst incident took place at Balham Underground station on 14 October 1940, when a bomb burst a water main and more than sixty people were drowned from the five

19   *The entrance to one of London's numerous underground stations, protected and converted into a public shelter. This one is at Mansion House.*

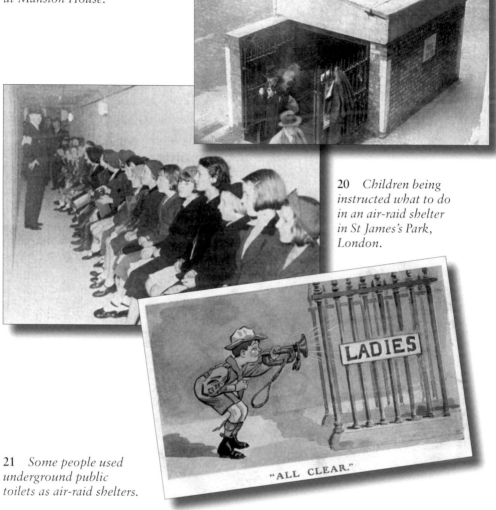

20   *Children being instructed what to do in an air-raid shelter in St James's Park, London.*

21   *Some people used underground public toilets as air-raid shelters.*

"ALL CLEAR."

hundred who sheltered there. Many more were also injured. Betty Parkyn, who was about 12 at the time, lived in Tooting, and an entry in her diary from 1944 states that she slept in the underground at Trinity Road, now Tooting Bec, and has the platform ticket as verification. Eventually many people chose to shelter in the cupboards under their stairs. These were remarkably strong and safe places to be. Photographs of bombed buildings reveal that the only structures left standing were often the staircase or fireplace.

Roy Stevens lived in the Dorset village of Broadstone near Poole and explains that the village itself was of no interest to the Luftwaffe, but it lay on their flight-path to major towns and cities inland. His sleep was constantly being disturbed by air-raid warnings and the unmistakable drone of enemy aircraft overhead. He describes how the family would 'shoe-horn' themselves into a tiny cupboard under the stairs, feeling perfectly safe, until the relief of the all clear. 'It was a standing family joke,' he claims, 'that I was more frightened of spiders than of the enemy above.' Their one moment of genuine danger occurred when an incendiary bomb set fire to a builders merchants paint store just along the lane. The store was completely gutted, its concrete base making a great football pitch for the local kids. At Wigston, Doreen Boulter's mother decreed that all the 'paraphernalia' under the stairs should be cleared out. 'Our under the stairs,' she describes, 'had a door to it.' It was situated in the middle of the house, so her mother thought it the safest place. 'We set to and cleared out the accumulation of many years,' continues Doreen. The 'paraphernalia' was then replaced by stools, a flashlight, candles, matches, a first aid box containing plasters and a bottle of iodine, and her father's cricket bat. This was a relic from the days when he played for Wigston Prims cricket team. Her mother insisted that it was to clout any German parachutists that dared to set foot in her house. When the sirens sounded, it was to this cupboard that the family made a beeline, including their dog Prince, a new addition to the family. A few weeks after war was declared, Doreen's father had brought it home from work. Her mother was 'none too pleased,' until her husband explained that one of his work mates had been called up and his wife had told him to get rid of the dog as she did not want the bother of it. Saved from being put down, the mongrel was installed in a wooden orange box underneath the treadle sewing machine and became one of the family. We can only surmise as to how many dogs and other pets were put down under similar circumstances as a consequence of war.

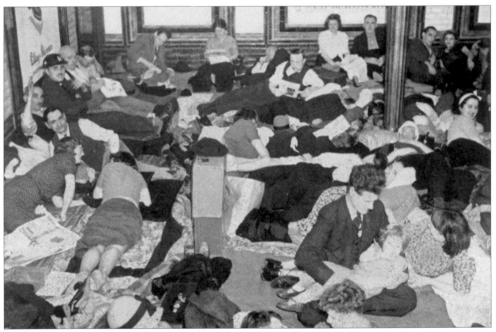

22   *Thousands of Londoners sought shelter in underground stations every night during the bombing, bringing their bedding and food with them.*

At the Anderson shelter in Doreen Govan's garden, things became too uncomfortable after a while and then their neighbour Sheila developed chicken pox, so it was agreed that the shelter would be abandoned and that everyone would be safer in the cupboards under their own stairs. Her mother and Mrs Upton developed a code to let each other know how they were. This was a system of knocking on the wall between their terraced houses. If people did not have Anderson shelters or cupboards under the stairs, they improvised. At Cayton near Scarborough, for instance, Jenny Peacock recalls that down one side of their kitchen were metal shelves attached to the wall. When the sirens sounded they simply sheltered beneath these.

In March 1941 the government began to issue shelters that could go inside people's houses called Morrison shelters. These were made of heavy steel and had wire mesh sides. They were named after Herbert Morrison, the Home Secretary, could be placed anywhere in the house, such as the living room or the kitchen and could double up as tables. One of the sides lifted up, enabling people to crawl into an area that provided sleeping space for two or three. At Eye in Suffolk, Joy Matthews (née Randall) remembers having one of these in the front room of their house. She describes it as being 'rather like a large rabbit hutch'. If the air-raid siren sounded this was their destination. However, when there was cause to use it one afternoon, the plan went somewhat awry.

> One afternoon Moaning Minnie the air-raid siren went off for the first time and just as we were making for the front room there was a loud knock on the door. An officious ARP warden insisted that we went to the public shelter about 500 yards away in a field. Under protest my mother locked the house collected her handbag and picked me up in her arms. It was too late; already the hum of an enemy aircraft could be heard, getting closer. As we went down the path at the side of the house a Jerry plane homed in on us, guns blazing. Well, only one gun really but that was enough. We could see his face he was that close. Miraculously the bullets missed us leaving pock-marks in the wall of the house. We didn't bother with the public shelter after that, far too risky.

Many people naturally utilised their Morrison shelter for a range of other purposes. You could eat your dinner from it, clean your shoes on it, or use it as a place to do your school homework. But surely the most unusual use is recorded by Margaret Harber from Swindon, whose cousin was actually born on her auntie's shelter.

Schools had mapped out drills for their students during air raids. At Broadstone, Roy Stevens recalls that shelters were built on part of the playground and when the air-raid siren sounded the children would take a book and troop down into the dank, dark interior until the all clear sounded. 'We never minded these excursions as it meant a break from lessons!' Audrey Purser lived in Down Road, Merrow, near Guildford, and attended Down Road School, which was in the same street. When the sirens sounded here, the children quickly made their way to the shelter in the playground and to keep their minds occupied, the teacher gave them pieces of toilet paper to draw on which had the texture of tracing paper. Jean Wells, who lived in the Merton Park area of London, remembers their school shelters being in the sports field. Their morale was maintained by singing. As the guns at the top of the road went into action, the singing got louder in order to drown out the noise.

In Norwich, Ron Green attended school at Crooks Place, today known as Bignold School. Here there were purpose-built shelters for older children, while for younger pupils like himself there was 'a make-shift job between two buildings'. Before Ron and his friends headed for their refuge, they were instructed to take a biscuit and a small cube of cheese to nibble. He admits that some children prayed for the siren to sound, in order to miss school and enjoy these impromptu goodies. They were also instructed to take a small piece of linen about an inch and a half square that had probably come from some old unwanted garment. 'Our job,' he explains, 'was to unweave the strands, and all these small strands would then go to fill pillows for the army or hospitals.' So, although the children were avoiding classes, they were being made to do war work to occupy their time.

In Brighton, where shelter drills were carried out regularly, Moya Knight explains that KitKats were used to lure children to safety. They were required to line up in columns of two, and then march in an orderly fashion into the shelter until everyone was sitting on the hard wooden benches along the sides. On route they were issued with a small packet of biscuits and a two-finger KitKat, which they were not allowed to eat for at least two hours. Moya recalls that on one occasion permission was granted to eat the biscuits, but the chocolate bars were never consumed. 'One boy actually ate his KitKat,' she notes, 'and was in terrible disgrace, held up to the school as a bad example!'

Iris Thomas explains that at her school at rural Boddington near Cheltenham, which only had about thirty pupils, the air-raid shelter was a small cloakroom stacked to the roof with sandbags. The children looked forward to hearing the sirens as it meant lessons would be abandoned. 'Thinking about it now,' she contemplates, 'if a bomb had landed nearby we would probably have been buried by the sandbags'. At Gravesend in Kent, Julie Baker says that her school shelter was also a back room lined with sandbags.

Some schools had no shelters at all. At Ammanford in south Wales, Myra Williams (née Jones) notes that children were evacuated to houses nearby if German planes were known to be in the area. Each child had a named house to which they were allocated, and once an air raid was announced he or she would make their way to that address. There were usually two or three children to each house, the theory being that if a bomb did hit the school, the children would not be all in one place. After the raiders had passed and the all clear was sounded, they would all return to school. The system was not confined to the countryside, and Margaret Ball describes how, during the air-raid drills at her school in Exeter, pupils were also dispersed around the neighbourhood. Each child was allocated a house and was told to go and stand on the doorstep. In the event of bombing the occupier was obliged to take them in. 'We did this drill regularly,' she confirms. At home they also had a Morrison shelter and Margaret clearly remembers cowering beneath this during the Exeter Blitz, while her youngest sister recited the Lord's Prayer, convinced that the next explosion would seal their fate.

At a Brighton school where the playground was unable to accommodate a shelter, seven-year-old Betty Field explains that their evacuation arrangements involved lining up outside the school and then running down the street for about one hundred yards to turn right into the local brewery yard. The route took them along a raised concrete path past a pit full of broken bottles and down a steep flight of stairs into a cellar. Here they spent many hours sitting on long, uncomfortable, wooden forms.

> The smell of the malt and hops was revolting. As I got older and realised the damage bombs could do, I thought we would all be cut to pieces by this glass or drowned in beer. The rules at school were, once in the shelter we could only leave in the middle of a raid if one of our parents collected us and took responsibility. My father was working and my mother was of an extremely nervous disposition, so she never ventured out. Hence I was always the last child left sitting in the shelter and when the brewery closed at 5.30pm the teacher and I were sent to a public shelter nearby. It was always the headmaster and I think he got fed up with never getting home on time, so ultimately when we were the last two he would walk me home. This was advantageous to me as he would sit and read to me or continue to teach me. This was education on a one-to-one basis which of course is priceless but I didn't realise it at the time.

In the village of Flimby, children were protected by nothing more than a hole dug in the ground. Ethel Fisher explains that if the teacher blew a whistle, they had to pick up their gas masks, which were kept under their desks, and march in lines out of school and across the road, while the teachers held up any traffic. Next they had to climb over a four foot high stone wall into a field, in the centre of which was a very large 'sand-hole'. Before the war, excavators would normally be seen here removing sand for building purposes but such work had ceased and the sand-hole was now redundant. Having reached it, each child had to find a hiding place and get under cover as quickly as possible. Sometimes the girls discovered that boys from a neighbouring school had beaten them to it. 'Being children we found all this to be great fun and very exciting, not realising the serious nature of the proceedings,' smiles Ethel. Today she appreciates the great responsibility that was put on the shoulders of her teachers during the war but, fortunately for both them and their pupils, Ethel never experienced a real air raid whilst at school.

The Black-Out
In order to minimise the danger from bombing, all homes and businesses were ordered to 'black-out'. All windows and doors had to be covered with something dark, such as curtains or wooden boards, to prevent any light escaping. Even then the use of lights or open fires were kept to a minimum in order to deter an ARP warden from banging on your door and ordering you to 'put that light out!'

In the city of Leeds, Molly Kinghorn remembers the black-out curtains made by her mother to cover all the windows. These had to be drawn before any lights were put on. Her father also made plywood covers for the cellar windows. At Broadstone, the father of Roy Stevens secured stout black paper to slim wooden frames that were then placed in the windows. People used their initiative, and whatever materials were available to them.

Barbara Raine from Bradford was staying with her family in Norfolk when the black-out was introduced. The household members gathered together old bedding,

23   Molly Kinghorn (front right) on the steps of her house in Leeds. Next to her is Joan Bennet, an evacuee adopted by her Auntie Dora. In the back are Molly's mother, grandmother and sister Joan. Molly recalls her mother making black-out curtains for all the windows. The railings outside the house would soon disappear.

curtains, table-cloths and drawing pins to cover all the windows. After Barbara had been put to bed, all the lights in the house were put on and the adults went out to the garden to test the effectiveness of their efforts. She could hear voices, and then her mother screamed. A bat, somewhat disorientated by the new arrangements, having flown into her back. In the morning Barbara's mother decided to return home to take care of her own black-out, so they packed and headed for the train station. 'The train journey was something of a nightmare,' describes Barbara. 'The station names had been removed or covered over, and all we were told was "This train is going north".' So we got on and hoped for the best. Happily, we did arrive safely at Bradford, after a bit of an ordeal.'

In the 1940s many domestic properties still had very basic systems for lighting and heating. They were already cold and dark at the best of times, so the black-out could cause great discomfort for young children. This point is made very clear by Marie Litchfield, who lived in a cottage in rural Somerset, where, even here, regulations had to be observed.

> Winters could be very cold. Houses were not centrally heated – were not in fact heated at all. The living-room would have its fire and once that was lit there was one warm room; the kitchen became warm while the cooking was being done. But there was no attempt at heating the other downstairs rooms or upstairs. If there was a new baby, or we were ill, Mother would light the old black Valor stove and bring it into our bedrooms for a while to give a little warmth as we undressed. Its light made exciting patterns on the ceiling of the dark bedroom. Although there were electric lights in the bedrooms, we could not afford bulbs most of the time. And in the war years there was no chance of using electric lights unless one had very meticulous arrangements for blacking out the windows, which we did not have. Even a tiny chink of light showing from the lane would bring an Air raid Warden to the door. The living-room had shutters, and in the kitchen it was quite easy to hang a blanket or an old coat over the window, so these rooms could be well lit. Tiny oil-lamps had to suffice for the hallway and bedrooms. I marvel now how we didn't have accidents in the dark as we went up and down the twisted stairway, with its steps narrowing to nothing as it rounded the corner.

Although they didn't use them, Marie's house in Somerset had electric lights, but at Merrow in Surrey, all that Audrey Purser's cottage could boast was one gas light in the main downstairs room. She describes how a piece of pipe that nearly

24   *Roy Stevens aged eight at his home in Broadstone, Dorset, where his father secured stout black paper to slim wooden frames that were then placed in the windows.*

reached to the ceiling came out of the floorboards, before arching out into the room. A glass light shade and a delicate mantel were attached to the end. The mantel was so delicate in fact that it would often break while being lit with a spill, and then had to be replaced. Upstairs they had no lighting at all, so the children used to take candles to bed. Audrey and her sister Sheila would take the candle out of the holder and pour the wax on to their hands and, after it had cooled, peel it off again. She found it rather 'spooky at night' with the dark curtains up, and her sister would frighten her with stories about ghosts floating in the air and coming out of the cupboard. In the winter it was so cold at night that, although her mother put two 'very thin' army blankets and her father's Home Guard overcoat on the bed, it was still not enough to keep them warm, and the sisters found it difficult to get to sleep. Like most houses at the time, Audrey's cottage had an outside toilet, where cut up old newspapers were used as toilet paper. It would get so cold that her father put an oil lamp in the toilet to stop the cistern from freezing. However, during the war, unable to use lights outside, the children had either to go before the black-out, or in complete darkness. Audrey explains that her sister always somehow managed to go first and afterwards

25   *Black-out. Placing metal discs over the traffic lights in Oxford Street.*

would say the toilet was full of spiders and other creepy crawlies. 'She knew I hated them. Of course I had to go out and went as fast as I could with the wind blowing the trees at the bottom of the garden. The branches would sway all over the place and the owls hooted. It was so scary for a young girl in the dark!'

At Avoch in the Black Isle, Donald Patience recalls how his brother got the fright of his life in the black-out. He was coming home in the pitch dark when something light brushed past him. Being a child he immediately thought it was a ghost, but it turned out to be a local lady wearing a light coat and soft soled shoes.

The black-out had to be observed even away from the cities, as enemy aircraft failing to locate their target were likely to drop their bombs on any light source they observed below. Also, sites supporting the war effort in some way could have been in very rural locations, so the twinkling lights of a nearby village or farm might have been all German navigators required to locate them. Boddington, for instance, where Iris Thomas lived, may have been in rural Gloucestershire, but it was very close to the Rotol Aircraft works at Staverton Airfield and several other possible targets. Iris explains that:

> Because of the aircraft factories the black-out was very important. Mr Carter, who worked with my father at the local manor, was also a local special police officer and was responsible for enforcing the black-out. My father was always very diligent at ensuring we had no light showing and was very indignant when one night Mr Carter tapped on the window and told us we did. My father invited him inside to inspect the property which Mr Carter could find no fault with. As it was a cold night my father offered him a glass of home made wine which he readily accepted. We then found that Mr Carter regularly needed to check our black-out, especially on cold nights!

Iris's father was too old to be called up, so one of his wartime jobs was to help light and maintain smoke generators that were used each night to produce a smoke screen to hide the aircraft factory. This usually meant having to stay out till dawn. In the mornings, when walking to school, Iris could still smell and taste the oily smoke in the air.

Doreen Govan notes that no street lights came on at night in Bristol. In an attempt to avoid accidents in the dark, lampposts were painted with white stripes, as were the sides of kerbs. People also protected their windows against the blast from bombs dropped nearby by sticking strips of brown paper across the windowpanes. Doreen Govan explains that 'this was to prevent windows being blown out by blast and the flying glass causing accidents'. For similar reasons her mother dutifully covered her beloved piano with an eiderdown every night.

Travelling by motor transport at night was to be avoided unless absolutely necessary, in which case the headlights on cars had to have special shields over them so that only a small amount of light pointed down towards the ground. Buses had their lights covered and a small beam of light from a hole was all the driver had to see his way. In Bristol the trams were removed, never to return again. People began to wear fluorescent armbands and strips on their clothing, and while batteries were still available, they were allowed to carry torches but, similar to the buses, had to cover the light leaving just a tiny pinhole to see by.

Some people were so poor in the 1940s they could not afford to light and heat their houses at all. Johnny Ringwood, who lived in the Custom House area of London, attended a school for malnourished children called Fyfield, which was owned by the old West Ham Council. Apparently half his street, Jersey Road, also went there. His father was in the army and his mother worked all day as a crane driver for Harland and Wolff in the docks. During the winters Johnny always felt really cold because of the lack of coal. His mother told him not to light the fire in the morning before going to school, but to wait until he came home later. This meant that when he got up in the morning their flat was like a fridge. Johnny would always go to school early so that he could get warm sitting by the fire in the cloakroom. There was no hot water at the flat, so washing oneself was very rudimentary and he describes 'a quick wash of the hands and face and that was about it'. When his mother came home from work she would check his neck to see if it had been washed, and if the evidence suggested that it hadn't he would receive a clip around the ear.

Chapter 3

An Island Fortress

After the evacuation of Dunkirk, the Germans had reached the Channel coast of France. At the narrowest point of the English Channel they were now only 21 miles away. In Britain people expected the enemy to keep coming, that an invasion was imminent. The entire kingdom became an island fortress as fortifications, guns and military camps appeared everywhere. For children the sight and sounds of troops, vehicles, aircraft and ships became part of daily life. Many people found themselves living close to army camps, airfields, naval bases or other wartime establishments, and for many children this was an exciting time to be alive, even though it was also fraught with danger.

The Military Presence

By 1940 almost every corner of Britain had a military presence and children became used to seeing service personnel virtually on their back doorstep. Margaret Harber was six years old and living in Leamington Grove, Swindon near the main road that led to the army camp at Chiseldon where, as at Eastville Park in Bristol, soldiers were camped after Dunkirk as they waited to rejoin their units. Many of them would be invited inside and regaled with a few home comforts. For a young girl, having soldiers in the house was very exciting, although Margaret now appreciates that it must have been an extremely anxious and frightening time for her parents. An invasion was likely at any moment.

Although Molly Kinghorn came from Leeds she spent a lot of time with her grandparents at Haverah Park, Beckwithshaw near Harrogate, an estate owned by Ripley Castle. Molly's grandfather, as well as being a tenant farmer, also worked for the estate as a woodman. There was an army camp nearby at Penny Pot Lane, so it was not unusual to observe soldiers on manoeuvres and sometimes they could be seen crawling around her grandfather's outbuildings. One day her mother noticed soldiers drinking water from the beck. She told them not to drink it, but did not like to give them the reason why, so the children took great delight in telling them that the contents of the farm toilet flushed directly into the water a little up stream. White enamel mugs were quickly put away.

Many new sites were taken over or built on, and in some places large buildings were requisitioned for military use. At Boddington Manor near Cheltenham, where the father of Iris Thomas worked, the manor was initially requisitioned by the Royal Army Service Corps and later by the Americans. Iris describes how local children would enjoy seeing soldiers being punished, running past her house in full kit followed by a sergeant on a bicycle. As they returned the children would

26   *Molly Kinghorn's sister Joan and cousin Michael playing beside the beck where the soldiers drank. The contents of the farm toilet flushed directly into the water a little up stream.*

shout encouragement to them. There was also a tent under a horse chestnut tree, used for solitary confinement, which appeared to be constantly occupied by a soldier playing a mouth organ who only knew one tune, *Home on the Range.* He would wave to any children that passed, and sometimes, if there were no guards in evidence, the kids would creep into the field and chat to him through the fence.

Every Sunday Iris and her family would attend Boddington's small Saxon church. The usual congregation numbered between 12 and 20 people and Iris herself belonged to the choir. However, after the manor was requisitioned the church was also used as the venue for the Royal Army Service Corps church parade

27   *The crew of an anti-tank gun look out to sea somewhere along the east coast of England.*

28 *'Saluting the victor' by Joe Crowfoot. Children wave to a Spitfire pilot, after he has dispatched an enemy raider into the English Channel.*

every other Sunday. The tiny church would soon fill up and soldiers would spill out into the porch. Sometimes members of the regimental band would attend and Iris recalls the fantastic difference this made during the singing of the hymns. The leader of the band was a man called Reg Harris and he organised ENSA shows to entertain the troops stationed at the manor. One night Iris's father returned home after one of these shows enthusing about a particular performer they later discovered to be a certain Norman Wisdom, who went on to great things after the war.

Many soldiers were billeted at Helston in Cornwall from Dunkirk until the end of the war. The first that Allan Thomas was aware of, shortly after the evacuation from France, were the Northumberland Fusiliers followed by the East Yorkshire Regiment. There were playing fields on the outskirts of Helston where children would observe these soldiers doing rifle drills and bayonet practise, or learning to ride army motorbikes, some with sidecars.

Allan's family were regular Sunday worshippers who would attend a chapel in Meneage Street. Many soldiers would attend the chapel and his parents would invite them home. One was a good pianist, so he and Allan's sister would play duets, while a couple of the others had good singing voices and would entertain the

29 *Iris Thomas would enjoy the sight of soldiers undergoing punishment running passed her house in full kit, followed by a sergeant on a bicycle.*

family. Later in the war, American soldiers stationed in the area would also attend the chapel and be invited to the house. After they left, their vacated tents were used to accommodate prisoners of war, some of whom would likewise find their way to the chapel and, in time to the Thomas house.

Bill Johnson lived in Bramley in Hampshire, which boasted a railway station on the Basingstoke to Reading line with the rather charming name of 'Bramley for Silchester'. This quiet village was surrounded by the military. To the south was a large ammunition depot and camps for both the Pioneer Corps and the Auxiliary Territorial Service. A little to the north, the Americans would turn Aldermaston into a large aerodrome for their B17 Flying Fortresses. Ammunition trains would constantly thunder along the railway line, keeping Bill awake at night, and the woods on the nearby country estate owned by the Duke of Wellington were used to conceal ammunition stores.

At Broadstone, Roy Stevens also experienced many sleepless nights as he lived about a mile away from an ordnance factory. In April 1941, in a bid to help food production, British Double Summer Time was introduced, which meant that it could be light until 11pm. That was fine for the farmers, but factories took advantage of the longer hours, too, leaving poor Roy lying in bed on hot summer evenings, unable to sleep as the machine guns were tested down the road.

Gerald Bartlett was born in Abbotsbury in Dorset in February 1939 and brought up by his parents in the nearby village of Portesham. The area's population was swelled by the military presence. Tank traps known as 'dragon's teeth' were all along Chesil Beach, placed as a precaution against a seaborne assault on the south coast, many of them still visible today. Convoys of lorries and tanks would trundle along the sea road. Motorcycle out-riders would station themselves at road

30   *The military presence was everywhere. A small boy looks on as soldiers and police check the identification papers of road users.*

31 *Molly Kinghorn would observe soldiers on manoeuvres crawling around her grandfather's outbuildings, a not uncommon sight in many parts of rural Britain.*

junctions to ensure the columns followed the correct routes. The first vehicle in the convoy would announce itself by flying a green flag, and you could tell when the last vehicle had passed because it flew a red one. Gerald explains that the convoys often encountered delays caused by herds of cows moving between the fields and the milking parlour or by sheep on their way to pastures new or to the sheep dips prior to their being shorn. There were very few tractors or other pieces of motorised farm equipment in Dorset in the 1940s, so most things were transported by slow-moving horses and carts. Steam-rollers were employed to flatten the ruts in the roads caused by military convoys.

In the early part of one afternoon when Gerald was about five years old a convoy of slow-moving tanks came down Portesham Hill and through the village. The primary school headmistress decided to keep all the youngsters behind, huddled around a coke fire with no food or drink until it had passed. Telephones were virtually non-existent, so parents could not be informed. Gerald does not know how long he was there, but it was dark when they were eventually allowed to leave. There were no street lights in the village, and as the pupils ranged from five to fourteen the older ones escorted the younger ones home. No one lived more than a mile away from the school, but the parents were enraged by the action taken by the headmistress and, according to Gerald, 'the rumpus went on for days'. In later life Gerald became a teacher himself and is certain the lady acted in the children's best interests.

Gerald's grandparents lived in Abbotsbury, a village noted for its narrow streets. The couple had a house at a junction, and on one occasion a tank driver failed to negotiate the turning and ploughed straight into the doctor's surgery opposite. Most of the building collapsed as the tank embedded itself in the masonry. Although one of the crew was killed and another badly injured, the surgery was empty at the time. The injured soldier was made comfortable in Gerald's grandmother's house before being taken to hospital in Weymouth. A couple of weeks later special equipment was used to pull the stricken tank from the debris. It was a difficult operation and all the houses surrounding the junction had to be evacuated.

In Merrow, a convoy of lorries fell foul of the winter weather, after snow fell heavily and lay deep on the Epsom Road. They were heading for the coast laden with troops and all the soldiers jumped off the lorries and ran along Down Road where Audrey Purser lived. She describes seeing the men in their long dark overcoats as both 'frightening and exciting'. They rushed up and down the road, calling at all the houses to find if there was anywhere two or more soldiers could spend the night. The following morning, after a lot of digging and pushing, and with all the local children watching, they managed to get moving again.

As the war went on, some soldiers became almost permanent fixtures and friends with the local children. Jacqueline Watson, who was born in 1935, lived in Brighton in a Victorian house that backed on to what was the Cox's Pill factory, now the site of a Sainsbury's supermarket. On the roof of the factory, was a machine gun, usually manned by two soldiers. As the months progressed these men became fond of the children and would throw chocolate into the garden for Jacqueline and her two-year-old brother. They would also come to the house asking if they could fill up their tea flasks. During the black-out Jacqueline would go into her bedroom and turn on the lights, until one of the soldiers pointed out that if the Germans got wind of this they would send their aircraft over to bomb her, and them. This frightened the girl so much that she turned the lights off immediately, and still walks around in the dark sometimes today.

During the entire course of the war the two men had only one opportunity to use their weapon in anger and, apparently, Jacqueline and her brother somewhat spoiled the moment. The children were playing in the garden when they heard a loud noise. The little boy pointed to the sky exclaiming 'big pane', of course meaning 'plane'. Jacqueline glanced up and saw a very low-flying aircraft, with a prominent cross on its fuselage. Their mother came running out to take them inside, but Jacqueline was only concerned about getting her dolly to safety. The scene quickly deteriorated into chaos, her mother screaming at her to 'leave the bloody thing', and the soldiers on the roof shouting for them to get under cover as they swung their machine gun into action. Years later, when speaking to an aunt about this incident, Jacqueline discovered that the aircraft in question had flown down Lewes Road shooting at anyone. Her aunt was doing her shopping and hid in a doorway, but what upset her most was the indignity of an old lady forced to throw herself into the gutter.

Military hospitals and convalescence centres were established all around the country, so another familiar sight for children at the time was wounded soldiers, some missing limbs or badly burned. Less than a quarter of a mile along the Epsom Road from Audrey Purser's house was a place called Merrow Grange. It had been a large hotel but was now turned into an auxiliary hospital. After their operations in Guildford servicemen were sent here to convalesce, although Audrey recalls that some minor operations were actually performed at the Grange itself. Looking down the drive of this imposing building, children could see nurses in white uniforms and starched white hats helping patients to walk around the beautiful gardens, other patients sitting on the seats in the sun. One of Audrey's friends belonged to the local Rangers, and took turns to make and serve the drinks to the patients and have a chat with them.

As well as army camps, the country quickly became covered with airfields. In Somerset, Marie Litchfield remembers an occasion when her father took her and her sister Bou on a long walk to the airfield at Weston Zoyland near Bridgwater. She can no longer recall the reason for the trip, but she does remember how the day almost ended in tragedy. Their home village of Ashcott sat along the Polden Hills and Marie remembers looking down on the airfield from the ridge as they progressed.

> It was a long walk but we were able to go right onto the runways and look at a couple of planes. A Spitfire was standing there for inspection – I think it must have been some kind of an open day, unless the men in charge were very lenient, because they let us climb into it. Before we left we saw, in another part of the aerodrome, a bomber loaded with bombs; and we knew it was destined to wreak havoc on some innocent town or village. We walked away from it, weighed down with heavy thoughts, and began to go across the runway in the direction of home. Then we became aware of a red light flashing on and off urgently. We calmly looked around, wondering what it was all about, then suddenly directly over our heads swept in a landing plane. We hadn't known it was coming because of the speed of its approach, but of course the control-tower had, and was frantically trying to warn us of our danger. We left soon after that – it was one of those near-disasters that happen so quickly that we don't realise their magnitude at the time. Afterwards we knew how lucky we had been.

Airfields appeared all over Britain, even in the most remote locations. On the Black Isle north of Inverness, where Donald Patience lived, there were numerous small ones, among them Blackstand, which was used by light aircraft such as Defiants. The children of the Black Isle would cycle over to have a look at these from time to time. Once a Swordfish biplane crashed just offshore, between Avoch and Fortrose, and Donald could see it on his way to and from school. On several occasions local fishermen used their boats to help rescue crews from aircraft that had gone down in the Moray Firth. Donald can also recall seeing RAF fighter aircraft training over the Firth by pretending to attack Blackburn Bothas employed as target planes. The Moray Firth was also buzzing with small naval vessels. 'It was exciting for young lads like myself watching the big flying boats taking off and landing,' he says. 'They sometimes flew low over our house and I would wave to the pilots as they went past.'

Ethel Fisher lived on a 500-acre farm called St Helens near Flimby in Cumbria. On one occasion two aircraft were passing overhead, which she believes were Spitfires, when one of them experienced engine failure. It subsequently nose-dived into the gateway of one of their fields. Half the population of Flimby came to see it followed shortly afterwards by ten soldiers from Carlisle Castle. These came to guard the stricken plane and, while there, lodged in the farmhouse. Ethel's family was allocated extra food rations, as the men had to be fed as well as accommodated. The soldiers remained on the farm for a fortnight, a period Ethel describes as 'a wonderful two weeks!' She could play the piano and two of the soldiers had mouth organs, so many were the sing-songs they had. But it wasn't all fun for these men, as they peeled potatoes by the bucketful and scrubbed the dairy floor. They even had a go at milking the cows, but did not master the art. Luckily it was harvest time and they also helped readily when not on guard. 'They were just as disappointed as we were,' says Ethel, 'when they had to return to barracks.'

In one of their fields contractors built a mock aerodrome made entirely out of wood. About one and a half miles away was an underground room with a switch-board, and when the air-raid sirens sounded buttons pressed here lit up the mock aerodrome. The purpose of this deception was to distract enemy planes away from the nearby steel works at Workington. 'The whole thing was manned by disabled ex-servicemen,' Ethel expands. These men also spent many hours in the farmhouse enjoying the home cooking. The dug out remains and is plainly visible from the main road between Maryport and Workington.

32   *Rosa Bowler and her grandfather with a bren gun carrier, resting in the family yard at East Ilsley while troops manoeuvred in the area in 1939-40.*

33   *With airfields being built all over the country, boys in particular took a great interest in the different types of aircraft seen in the skies of Britain, and aircraft identification books became all the rage. This is the cover of one of a series of booklets published by* The Aeroplane *in 1943.*

34   *Cover of a wartime booklet published by Hutchinson & Co., illustrating all the ships of the Royal Navy. Another schoolboy's 'must have'.*

Changing Landscape

As well as the many military camps being established to accommodate or train service personnel, the landscape around British towns and cities was changing. Anti-aircraft guns, searchlights and barrage balloons would become familiar to children in the years ahead and were concerned with protecting the nation against air attack.

Anti-aircraft – or ack-ack – gun emplacements were just as likely to be found at the end of the street, or in a park, as they were around a military establishment, especially in London and other major cities. These guns worked in synchronisation with searchlights and were components of a much larger, sophisticated detection system. Once an enemy aircraft had been located the searchlights would illuminate the target, enabling the guns to destroy it. The guns were usually situated in a sand-bagged emplacement and their crews would become familiar faces to local people. Doreen Govan recalls that all the hills and high ground in Bristol were commandeered by the War Office and the gun emplacements built on them were fenced off with barbed wire and out-of-bounds to civilians.

Although anti-aircraft batteries were dangerous pieces of ordnance for enemy aircraft, the one installed near the north London home of Gerald Lettice, actually caused him to wind up in a hospital bed. It was stationed in a local sports field and placed off-limits to excited young boys, so in order to get a closer look he cycled down a nearby road and stood up on the pedals to view the 'gleaming green gun barrels with their shiny metal tips'. So overawed was he at the sight that he failed to notice an obstruction in the road and the next thing he remembers was waking up in hospital, having sailed over the handlebars and suffered cuts, bruises and concussion.

Gerald Webb was born in 1933 and lived at Fareham in Hampshire just under Portsdown Hill, which has six old forts on it built in the 1800s to protect Fareham and Portsmouth. The army established ack-ack positions in each, to upgrade the defences of the area in line with the current threat. When these guns went into action, Gerald found the noise was immense. The whereabouts of these pieces of ordnance also attracted the attention of someone he considered an enemy spy. 'I remember as a boy walking in the woods with a friend,' he ponders, 'when out of some bushes came a man in an army uniform, but with no badges.' In their young eyes he was a German spy because he was tall and blond, and he borrowed some binoculars they carried, explaining that he wanted to observe his mate who was on sentry duty at Fort Wallington. 'We did not believe it then and I do not now,' says Gerald. 'We followed him at a safe distance until he walked away out of Fareham. We did not have the courage to tell a policeman about our suspicions, as we were frightened of them in those days, unlike the youth of today, so I shall never know if he was genuine or not.'

There were several types of anti-aircraft gun, and several types of ammunition used, one causing a bit of a stir when it was tested along the Kent coast. Frank Stanford, who was living at St Margaret's at Cliffe near Dover, left the house one morning to find the place strewn with strips of metal about two inches wide and six feet long. They could be seen hanging from roofs and trees, or just lying across lawns and roads. Chimney pots had been knocked over, and roof tiles were broken and on the ground. According to Frank:

> Our parents were told that the Royal Artillery had been trying out a new explosive shell. The shell head was packed with light coils of flat wire, like the spring in a clock. So when the shell exploded this wire would fly into the propellers of aircraft so bringing them down. Of course the idea was a good one, but only over sea and not land. I often wondered how they managed to wind this flat wire into the head of an explosive shell.

As a footnote to this story, for several years Frank has written articles for his parish magazine. In one such article he mentioned these shells and, to his surprise, received a letter from a gentleman who had the job of putting the metal into the shell heads. They were never widely used and discontinued after a few experiments, but Frank can at least confirm that what his parents had been told was true.

Searchlights were located everywhere, and not just with anti-aircraft batteries. Their intense beams of light would scour the heavens in search of their quarry. Even in rural Somerset Marie Litchfield describes how, 'at night, after dark, we would lean out of the bedroom windows and watch the long fingers of the searchlight beams criss-crossing and feeling about in the sky as they tried to locate planes overhead. We used to hope they would miss them'. At Ammanford in Wales, Myra Williams remembers the searchlights set up on Betws Mountain, their lights dazzling the enemy pilots and preventing them from locating the Skewen Oil Works, which was among their targets in the area. However, if they were successful ordinary people would be in danger. Incendiary bombs were once dropped on an in-law's farm making large craters and starting fires after the Germans had failed to locate the oil works. At Axmouth, June Richards watched as aircraft crossing the coast became caught in the beam of the searchlight at the top of the village. Aircraft were passed from one searchlight to another along the coast, until eventually an ack-ack battery would have it in its sights, and the sound of artillery fire would be heard.

Just up the road from the farm near Glentham in Lincolnshire where Mary Cooper lived with her mother, sister, grandparents and uncle was a large house called The Chestnuts. A searchlight unit was situated here and her grandmother would often cook supper for the airmen who manned it. They provided her with all the provisions and would also bring chocolate and 'lovely slab cake' for Mary and her sister, who would stand at the top of the stairs long after they should have been in bed, eager to see what the men had brought them.

Barrage balloons were another familiar wartime sight to children. They hung in the sky over the approaches to factories and other vulnerable sites and were tethered to winches by metal cables. They were designed to protect the sites from the attack of low-level aircraft or dive-bombers. Marie Litchfield describes them as looking 'quite grotesque', while Doreen Govan likens the barrage balloons of Bristol to 'great grey elephants', that soon appeared in the sky over the city. 'Every available patch of grass, had its own defensive measure,' she writes. 'Not a park nor a playing field was without its tethered balloon and its accompanying Nissen hut with complement of RAF personnel. Ours was on Packer's Field, which was also the grammar school playing fields. I was to attend that school for the next five years.'

35   *An anti-aircraft gun mounted in a London park, with sandbags being placed around it*

At Boddington, Iris Thomas recalls the excitement when a stray barrage balloon somehow became untethered from its winch and landed in a nearby field. 'We all went down to see it,' she states, 'and found that most of the villagers were cutting off bits of the balloon for souvenirs.' Iris herself acquired a piece of the monster and kept it for many years to come.

36 *Barrage Balloons were a familiar sight to the children of wartime Britain.*

37 *A searchlight scours the heavens in search of enemy aircraft.*

Chapter 4

A Land of Uniforms

Other than those in reserved occupations, or forced to work in essential services like the Bevin Boys who laboured in the coal mines, the male population of Britain volunteered or was conscripted into the armed forces. This meant that a large proportion of children spent the war years without a father figure. In fact, many children had practically no male influence at all, as their uncles, cousins, older brothers and sometimes even grandfathers were serving in the Army, Royal Navy or Royal Air Force. Others served in the Merchant Navy, which became known as the fourth service. Everywhere you looked people were in uniform, not only male members of the family, but often the women as well, and the streets flooded with servicemen from around the world.

A Nation in Uniform

As a bank clerk the father of Frank Hind was in a 'reserved occupation'. He did not have to join the armed forces and could remain safely at home with his family, continuing in his pre-war occupation. Other reserved occupations included dock workers, miners, farmers, scientists, merchant seamen, railway workers, medical practitioners, police officers, school teachers and utility workers, considered essential to the war effort. Men in these positions were still able to do their bit for the country by joining a branch of the Civil Defence and became ARP wardens, auxiliary firemen or special constables. However, Frank's father, like many other men in his position, still felt he should join the army and support his country by fighting instead. He was 37 at the time, and after gaining permission from his employer, Westminster Bank, enlisted in the Somerset Light Infantry as a private in 1941. His family did not see him again until the spring of 1946 when he was demobbed with the rank of major, having been commissioned into the Pioneer Corps, and seen active service in North Africa and Italy. Frank's mother had to bring up both him and his autistic brother on her own. She managed extremely well and Frank admits that 'Strangely, they were happy times.'

In Devizes, Bill Underwood's brother Peter joined the Royal Navy in 1941, and Arthur, the man who worked in his father's barber's shop, joined the army. So, in order for the business to survive, Bill entered the world of hairdressing on a part-time basis at 12 years of age. He was soon helping out during lunch hours, evenings and on Saturdays. Hair creams were in short supply so one of his jobs was to help manufacture them from ingredients his father obtained from the local chemist. But what Bill particularly enjoyed was making hairsprays using little more than a bottle of Tizer and a bucket of water.

All too infrequently fathers would come home on leave. Deanna Allan's father was in the Royal Navy and the occasions when he spent a few precious hours with his family were rare.

> One such visitation was unsanctioned and highly irregular. His unit had stopped for an overnight stay at Peterborough. The temptation of being just twenty-three miles from home was too much for Dad and he hitched a lift back to Corby to see his wife and girls. Instead of being delighted Mum was hysterical in case the military police realised he had gone AWOL. But he made it back to join his unit without incident. Perhaps his superiors turned a blind eye. On another occasion, 15 July 1944, when Dad was on leave our little family made the trip to Northampton by bus, to have our portrait taken by a studio photographer. Copies were given to both grandmothers and it was a photo Dad treasured all his life. I suppose it was something Mum would have if he did not return.

The uncle of Donald Patience was a captain in the Merchant Navy who once visited Avoch while on leave because his own wife and children had moved to the village from Sunderland and were renting a house there. During his visit he took Donald and his cousins on a trip to Invergordon, but they caught the wrong train. They soon discovered their mistake and got off again at a place called Achterneed, near Strathpeffer. The hapless mariner ushered the children into the waiting room, cautioning them to 'watch the step'. 'We managed fine,' smiles Donald, 'but he, resplendent in his captain's uniform covered in gold braid, fell flat on his face!' But the captain must have done something right during the course of the war because he was later awarded an MBE.

Many families lost loved ones prematurely, which meant that for a large number of children there would be no father figure in their lives after the war had ended either. People learned of their loss in many ways, Bill Underwood recalling that in April 1943 his cousin Ralph who served in the RAF was reported missing. Many people listened to the wireless broadcasts made by British fascist William Joyce, who became known as Lord Haw-Haw. These were initially transmitted from Berlin and began with the words 'Germany Calling, Germany Calling.' As well as disseminating Nazi propaganda he would read out the names of airmen who had been killed or captured. One night he read out Ralph's name, who had been killed over Denmark.

At Axmouth, June Richards had many members of her extended family serving in the armed forces. In the village was a telegram boy

38   *Frank Hind's father was in a reserved occupation, but he felt he should join the army and support his country by fighting instead. Frank is seen here with his father in June 1941.*

39   *Deanna Allan (née Dixon) and her family in Northampton on 15 July 1944. Deanna is on the right, aged three, with her sisters Jennifer (aged six, in the middle) and Dorothy (aged five, on the left), with their mother Agnes and father, Stoker Jack Dixon of the Royal Navy.*

who she considered looked 'nice' in his uniform. He would be seen cycling along the street and adults always appeared to be concerned about where he was going. 'It wasn't as nice to see him as I thought,' explains June, 'as he seemed to bring sadness to the houses at which he called.' He once came to her grandmother's house to deliver news that her son, June's Uncle Stan, had been wounded when HMS *Illustrious* was sunk and was on his way home. 'She died not long after that,' June relates, 'and I remember it being very sad.' The telegram boy came again to say that June's Uncle Herb was missing after HMS *Exeter* was sunk in the Battle of the Java Sea. He later returned with another communication, explaining that Herb was a prisoner in Japan where he remained until the end of hostilities, when a final telegram announced that he was safe in Canada.

At Sandend in Banffshire, Bruce Kean's uncle was employed by the Post Office as one such telegram boy. It was his job to deliver telegrams to families informing them about the loss of their loved ones. Mr Kean describes how he was once given the painful task of delivering a telegram to his own mother, telling her of the loss of one of her sons, the lad's own brother. He was one of four. 'How insensitive was that?' asks Mr Kean. His mother watched the boy as he walked up the garden path in a daze, thinking he was drunk. Carol was just seventeen, a boy telegraphist on HMS *Galatea*. Just a month earlier he had sent a Christmas card which, together with his last letter home, arrived after the 'missing presumed dead' telegram. He was never found and his mother had the grim task of informing her other two sons, one in the army and the other in the navy.

For Jean Wells, who lived in the Merton Park area of London, it was the sad loss of her mother that led to the most poignant memory she has of her father, who in 1942 was called up to serve in the RAF. Jean's mother became ill and subsequently died in September of that year and her father had to leave within six weeks of this tragic loss. While he was away, his children were cared for by two of his sisters, who were themselves working in a munitions factory. Trying not to be a burden to their aunts, the children did as much for themselves as they possibly could and endeavoured to help around the house. One thing that will stay with Jean forever, is the memory of sleeping in an air-raid shelter. 'It was mainly full of children,' she recollects, 'and you had to be there by a certain time, and were not allowed out again until about 7am. I saw my Dad coming towards the shelter that morning, in his RAF uniform, having just come home for a spot of leave. I ran up to him and he was crying.' Shortly after this event he was posted overseas, and it must have been extremely difficult being wrenched away from his children at such a distressing time in his own life.

Rosa Bowler (née Hibbert) lived in the village of East Ilsley in Berkshire. Her father joined the army quite early and being posted away became something of a distant figure. As a little girl she was very keen on horses and among her most cherished wartime possessions are the 'aerogrammes' that her father sent her from India at Christmas time. A friend of his was an amateur artist who would illustrate them with different equestrian scenes.

Mothers sometimes moved house to be with their uniformed husbands, even if it was only on a temporary basis. When Sylvia Cowcill (née Brown) was two years old in October 1939, her father volunteered to join the army and ended up serving with the Royal Engineers on the RAF base at Duxford. Her mother took her daughter and month-old baby son to be with their father, sharing a bungalow with a pilot and his wife who had a son of their own called Robert, about the same age as Sylvia. She has few memories of Duxford, other than a vivid recollection of her father in uniform taking her for a ride on the handlebars of his bicycle. And the incident with the beetroot! One day she and Robert were in the kitchen of the bungalow, and the table was covered with beetroot. 'Some had been peeled ready to go into vinegar,' she explains. 'Robert and I decided to tuck in. Robert's mum came in and said "Who's been eating the beetroot?" We both said we had not. Then I looked at Robert and at the same time he looked at me. We were both covered in beetroot juice. Busted!'

40   *Jean Russell, the little girl swinging on the hand of the Queen, was the daughter of one of many sailors who lost their lives during the Battle of the River Plate, on 13 December 1939, aboard HMS* Exeter. *She is seen here with her mother at Horse Guards Parade, as the King and Queen talk to relatives of those who died.*

41   *A hand-painted birthday card sent to Pamela Gear from her father in the RAF. She admits to having no idea who the artist was.*

Jean Hamer was seven when her father joined the army as a lorry driver, and shortly found herself moving to Scotland to be with him. When he first went away, her mother took on three separate jobs to survive. She worked in the Bicky Pegs Factory, a soup factory, and cleaned a school in the evenings. After her father returned from Dunkirk and was sent to Stirling his wife decided to join him, so the family stayed in lodgings. Jean attended the local school but admits to having difficulty in understanding both the teachers and the other children. So when her father was later posted to the Shetland Isles, they decided to move back to Welwyn Garden City. Jean lost her paternal grandparents in the bombing of Camberwell and says, 'I was still young enough not to be upset by it all, but how my father must have suffered!'

Many mothers took on the role of joint parents, but at the same time did their bit for the war effort. Some women joined the armed forces, while others did voluntary or charity work or worked in munitions factories or with the Women's Land Army. It was a difficult time for young mothers, and most children at some point were affected by their war work. In Leeds, for instance, the mother of Molly Kinghorn decided that the best way for her to 'do her bit' was to become a tram conductress for Leeds City Transport. 'We soon got into tram talk,' says Molly, mentioning terms like 'earlies, lates, splits and snivels'. Her father was very proud of his wife, and with the same pride he had taken in his own appearance during the First World War he would spend hours polishing her buttons, cash bag, hat badge and shoes. 'As all the windows were covered in netting' relates Molly, 'Mum had to shout out all the stops, so people knew where they were. As she had a rather refined voice it sounded a bit funny, but as she was brought up in Harrogate she was always reminding us to speak properly and not to use common Leeds talk.'

42   *Molly Kinghorn's mother in her tram conductress uniform in Leeds. Note how the head light of the tram has been shielded.*

43 *Cover of a wartime booklet, published by Raphael Tuck & Sons Ltd., entitled* The Home Front. *The illustration gives us a good impression of some of the Civil Defence and other jobs that mums, dads, and other adult members of the family might have done in uniform at the time.*

Many of the men unable to join the armed forces because they were in reserved occupations, or were too old, or too young, or had medical impairments such as colour blindness or flat feet, still wished to join the services, and their dreams were partly granted when in May 1940 Anthony Eden inaugurated the Local Defence Volunteers (LDV), which later became known as the Home Guard. The response to Mr Eden's initial broadcast asking for volunteers exceeded all expectations. The government had hoped to enlist around 150,000, but by the end of May, some 300,000 citizens had come forward.

As dads joined the new force, it seemed to many children as though they now had a real soldier in the house, complete with uniform and rifle. At Axmouth, the father of June Richards had volunteered for the army but was rejected on medical grounds, because of a wound he had sustained in the First World War. For old soldiers like him the LDV was a godsend. They were now able to be part of the war effort in a true military sense, taking care of the defence of both homeland and family at the same time. Mr Richard's duties included walking to a hut on the cliffs, from where he and another member of the LDV kept a sentinel watch on their stretch of the English Channel.

Members of the Home Guard did a wide variety of jobs in civilian life. Bill Underwood lists the members of his father's platoon, some of whom he occasionally brought home for a drink after training. One was Captain Weaver, manager of the local branch of Lloyds Bank and organist and choirmaster of St Mary's Church. Bill knew him well because he was for a while a member of the choir himself, for which he was paid three shillings a quarter, plus another shilling if he sang at a funeral.

Another Home Guardsman was Betty Field's father, who was too old to go into the forces. Her family lived in Brighton near two large bus garages and her dad worked for the bus company. The War Office decreed that in the event of invasion the buses would be vital to the enemy so the Home Guard had to be on duty every night to protect them. 'As we lived so near we were allocated rations for the Home Guard,' states Betty. 'Every night at about 7pm one of us would take the rations to the guard room. I think it was one ounce of tea, one pint of milk, four Oxo cubes and two ounces of sugar.' Each night these items would be weighed and placed in a large Oxo tin for transporting to the men. Once every hour a sentry would walk from one of the garages to the other, passing Betty's house on the way. Some of the lads were only 16 or 17 years old, and local girls would wait along their route intent on sidetracking them. This was usually stopped by the duty sergeant bawling at them at the top of his voice.

At Wigston, Doreen Boulter recalls that her father enlisted on hearing the appeal for volunteers on the wireless, and came home with an armband embroidered with the letters LDV. Her mother took one look at this and cynically snapped 'What are you going to do with that if the Jerrys come? Choke 'em with yer armband?' He explained that once they were better organised they would be equipped with proper uniforms and rifles, but for the moment they would be armed with shotguns, pitchforks and any other nasty implements they could muster. 'The idea of Father and the rest of his platoon standing up to fully trained German paratroopers brought on an outburst of unseemly mirth,' writes Doreen. No one in their right minds ever believed that Jerrys would ever set foot in Wigston'.

Before long her father was issued with a battledress top, and a week or so later he came home with trousers and a forage cap. He was appointed one of the platoon medics and wore an armband sporting a red cross. As well as regular training and manouvres, his platoon helped guard the canal bridge at Kilby Bridge and The *Navigation* pub. Then, on 7 September 1940, the Home Guard was mobilised and fathers were gone all night. It seemed as though the invasion was imminent and the signal for this, 'Cromwell', was flashed to units everywhere. Families waited with baited breath, but the invasion never came and the Home Guard was stood down, its members making their weary way home.

Soldiers from around the World

As Britain became more militarised, children came into contact with soldiers from many other parts of the world. At Huggate in Yorkshire, for instance, the area was used for tank training purposes, and John Hoggard and his friends had hours of fun watching the huge monsters ploughing up the fields and going through the hedges. Among the soldiers they encountered were Free French, who taught them snippets of their language, including how to ask for chocolate.

44 *School boys holding toy revolvers pretend to be invaders as Mr Churchill watches a Home Guard exercise in a Yorkshire village.*

Norwegian soldiers were stationed in the village of Avoch, and Donald Patience describes them as being very smart. One memory that has always stuck in his mind was watching them perform 'a strange form of high jump', which he later discovered was the Eastern Cut Off style. There were also Polish soldiers around Avoch known as French Poles because they had come from France at the start of the war; presumably they had been living and working there. 'Anyway, they certainly spoke French,' confirms Donald, who tried to communicate with them using his schoolboy knowledge of the language. On one occasion he persuaded one of them to do his French homework, expecting to achieve high marks but the man's English must have been on a par with Donald's French because he got his worst mark ever.

At Wallasey, Maureen Goffin's father worked in Liverpool Docks, and one of the Dutch ships there was unable to return to Holland as the country was now under Nazi occupation. One particular lad, named Cor, was confined to the ship because at 18 he was too young to be given shore leave while abroad. Maureen's father talked to the captain and signed papers to say he would be responsible for him if he went ashore, so Cor spent most of his free time with the family. Maureen's parents taught him to speak English and he remained in Britain after the war, marrying a girl from Southampton.

At Whitchurch in Shropshire, a place that would have been close to Hitler's proposed site of government in Bridgnorth had he successfully invaded Britain, Joyce Copper describes her house as being a 'cosmopolitan meeting place'. The town was surrounded by military hospitals, prisoner of war camps, small airfields and an American Army Air Force radio station and men of many nations became familiar visitors. Among those entertained were Jamaican airmen, one of whom became a Justice of the Peace in Birmingham after the war. Polish servicemen came in the evenings to play table tennis or sit by the fire and chat. All the servicemen would help her father, who was in a reserved occupation, in the garden, and generally made themselves useful when they had spare time. A Polish gentlemen who had been a saddle-maker produced the most wonderful hand-stitched school satchel.

The Americans soldiers, were here to train in readiness for the campaign to liberate occupied Europe, or to take part in the strategic bombardment of Nazi targets on the continent. Many parts of Britain were affected and by the end of the war almost three million GIs had passed through the country. It is estimated that in Suffolk alone there was one GI for every six civilians by D-Day, and American air bases had an enormous impact on local children.

45   *Cor on the left and his friend Joe, who served on the same Dutch ship. Being 18 years old, Cor was confined to the ship until the father of Maureen Goffin, who worked in Liverpool Docks, signed papers taking responsibility for him while ashore.*

At his home near Taunton, Frank Hind was influenced by the Americans even before they arrived. He was crazy about aeroplanes and spent many hours drawing pictures of them. Some cereal packets had war planes printed on them, for boys to cut out and assemble. On his eighth birthday his mother gave him what would become his prized possession, an official aircraft recognition manual, which he still has today. He soon memorised all of the aircraft contained in its pages, and one of his favourites was the 'L-5 Sentinel monoplane fixed undercarriage US Army liaison'. By 1944, the Americans were all around Taunton and Frank was thrilled to see this little plane overhead quite often, 'no doubt,' he imagines, 'ferrying senior officers to liaison meetings'.

46 *Of all the foreign soldiers who came to Britain, the Yanks had the biggest impact on local children. These smart GIs were based in an American hospital at Axminster in Devon.*

'I also admired the US vehicles,' he continues, 'the ubiquitous Jeep and the six wheeled trucks, even if the loud hiss of their brake hydraulics did rather startle me. That summer the GIs gave us rides in their Jeeps at the village fete, sometimes they would stop and give us rides at anytime. We kids loved them.' But it was not all 'sweetness and light'. Across the farmyard from their back door lived a family of farm labourers who had a daughter of around sixteen. She became pregnant by her coloured GI boy friend. 'That sent the hens a-cackling, including Mum!' he says. 'The poor girl was sent away to have the baby but I remember seeing her with it later on.' One night the Hind household was woken by a furious hammering on the front door, which turned out to be a drunken officer who had taken a fancy to Frank's mother, although he is quite certain she gave him no encouragement. The police were called and MPs arrived to cart him away.

One of the most profound impacts of the American invasion on children, was the contact with so many black soldiers. In 1939 there were roughly 7,000 black people in Britain, but by D-Day there were 500,000 Afro-Americans. Many people witnessed racial prejudice, and the segregation still prevalent in some parts of the USA. The first black American soldiers Bill Underwood saw were stationed at Bromham, a village three miles from Devizes. Black and white troops lived in separate camps, so rarely met but on their first foray into town there was a fight between the groups. Black soldiers were only permitted into Devizes one night a week thereafter, and on that particular evening the white soldiers were confined to quarters.

Doreen Govan describes how, in Bristol, the arrival of whole companies of black soldiers came as a culture shock. 'Remember hardly anyone in Bristol had ever seen a black person,' she says in their defence. According to Doreen, there were now two groups:

> Yanks and black Yanks. One day a company of these black soldiers came to Packer's factory, near our house, to be temporarily billeted before moving on. They sprawled along the pavements waiting to be let in and were a great entertainment to many of us local kids who were drawn to them like magnets. Very generous they were too, handing out dozens of packets of chewing gum, candy bars and American coins. One of them gave me a silver dollar with a hole in the middle for good luck, but someone swiped it off me at school.

In Testwood, about ten miles west of Southampton, Anne Biffin who was five when the war began admits that black GIs were regarded almost like novelty acts at the circus by some children. She describes how they were snapped up like hot cakes and taken home to meet mums and dads. She encountered one such GI when he was invited to the house of a school friend and other children, including herself were encouraged to come and meet him. 'I can see him now,' she says, 'a quiet gentleman looking very smart in his GI uniform sitting at a table playing cards, while we grubby little white kids gazed at him in awe.'

For people in Britain the war years had been austere, with rationing of many items, but when the generous Americans arrived, for some lucky people there was now an abundance of different food. At Bramley in Hampshire, Bill Johnson explains that his family never went short of things like butter, jam, tins of spam, and of course sweets for him with the GIs around. Much of Salisbury Plain and Wiltshire in general was given over to the American army and Devizes became the home of the 4th Armored Division. Bill Underwood's neighbour, Mr Hiscock, had a job as a stoker at one of the many local camps. One night, after finishing his late shift, he knocked on their back door some time after 10pm. He had walked down from the camp, which was about one and a half miles away, with a large container of ice-cream. There were no fridges, so it had to be eaten straight away. At the start of the war Bill was one of eight children, but by this time his mother had given birth to another two, so he was now one of ten. His mother raced upstairs and woke all the younger members of the family, in order for them to share in this special midnight treat.

Favours could sometimes be returned. At Axmouth, June Richards recalls how her father was always bringing American soldiers to the house for dinner.

We always had lots of meat as we kept pigs and poultry. My Dad always grew his own food so there was no problem. In the end we had six regular visitors. We had one very happy Christmas when there was twenty-two of us for dinner. The children ate theirs first and then the grown ups. We kept an eye on our guests, as we knew my Dad was going to surprise all the Americans. It was roast goose and this particular one had four wings. The surprise on their faces I shall never forget. They were lovely men, there was Big Mac, Little Mac, Leon, Tex, Hank and Warfey. I think it must have been the first time I tasted ice-cream. The soldiers had to go to Chard to collect it, but I remember it being very nice.

Compared to British soldiers the Americans were very well paid, so it was not long before children discovered methods to take advantage of them. The largest GI camp near Doreen Govan comprised the hundreds of Nissen huts and brick buildings erected to house troops on a large triangle of land at Frenchay. Some of these buildings would later become the famous Frenchay Hospital. The Americans would provide Doreen and her friends with the money to buy beer at the off-licence, for which they would be rewarded with candy. The proprietors never once asked their age. As soon as her mother found out about this she was stopped: 'I think she must have been heartily relieved that I was a skinny, flat-chested near fourteen-year-old and unlikely to attract the amorous attentions of any US soldiery. Going out with a Yank became a national pastime for any girls teenaged and upwards, often with disastrous consequences.'

47   *Mr and Mrs Hiscock, Bill Underwood's neighbours in Devizes. Mr Hiscock worked as a stoker at one of the American camps and would sometimes bring the children next door things like tinned fruit and ice-cream.*

48   *In this painting by Joe Crowfoot, two school children find themselves dwarfed by B-26 Marauders of the 322nd Bomb Group of the United States Army Air Force, based at Bury St. Edmunds.*

From Ash in Somerset, Shirley Copley attended a party for local children at the American base at Houndstone Camp in Yeovil. The Yanks were famous for throwing such parties, particularly at Christmas. However, as there were many schools in the area, it was decided on this occasion that only a handful of children could attend from each. The number depended on the size of the school, and only four children were selected from Ash school. A draw was held and Shirley was one of those chosen. On the day itself an American army lorry came to collect her and she remembers being a little afraid of having to sit next to a black soldier in the back as it was the first black person she had ever come across. That aside, she admits that it was a 'super party with films and lots to eat'. The only drawback was that she returned home with fleas!

Dion Copley recalls that Frome in Somerset was full of soldiers throughout the war and towards its end their numbers were increased greatly by the presence of the Americans, even Longleat House being used as a hospital. Many Americans were stationed around the town and the local children were always cadging gum from them. Some children also ran errands and were usually paid in gum and sweets. In Bath Street there was an American Red Cross canteen of which Dion's aunt was the manageress. It was known locally as the 'Donut Dugout'. The fat could only be used for so many doughnuts and then had to be discarded, so the staff would take it home for their families. Dion has a clear memory of food at home, particularly meat, having a distinct vanilla flavour.

49 *A Christmas party for the children of a local orphanage was held at the American airbase at Rattlesden in Suffolk in 1944.*

At Whitchurch, some of the American servicemen working at the Army Air Force radio station came to stay at Joyce Copper's house. Her mother helped out in the local Red Cross canteen, and after discovering that some of the soldiers were staying in very poor quality digs invited them to stay at her house. 'It was a good job they worked in shifts,' notes Joyce, 'because we didn't have much spare room.' One of the GIs stayed with them for three years, and during that time met and married a local girl. Joyce's mother used the money she was paid by the American Army for taking him in to pay for the wedding reception, which was held at the *Witchball Hotel*, Prees Heath.

While the Americans were staying at her house, Joyce reflects that life 'was never dull'. Along with her sister and brother she was spoilt terribly, fantastic food parcels being sent by families back home in the States. Going to school in a Jeep on some days was one of the highlights of this period. However, the saddest and most enduring memory she now has, is of a young paratrooper with the 101st Airborne Division who visited them before going to France on D-Day, where his forehead was seared by a bullet. The wound was not very serious and he visited them again in Shropshire while he recuperated. Once he was well again he went back to his unit and took part in the ill-fated operation to capture Arnhem in September 1944. It was here that he was killed and his father came to England in order to take his body home for burial. 'He was only 21 years of age and a truly nice young man,' concludes Joyce, 'and only one of a multitude of Americans, little more than boys, who gave their lives for this country.'

The Enemy Within

We have mentioned the many foreign soldiers with whom children came into contact, but more surprising is the fact that many also came into contact with the enemy in the form of German or Italian prisoners. There were many prisoner-of-war camps dotted all over Britain, and for all but a few, the prisoners' lives were relatively happy ones. There was discipline, in the form of roll calls every morning and night, but generally speaking life was much better for them than it was for British soldiers held by the Germans, Italians and Japanese.

With a severe shortage of manpower to perform seasonal tasks, as the foreign prisoners became more trustworthy they began to appear in the countryside helping out during harvesting, haymaking, and at other critical times. At Bramley, Bill Johnson notes that a great many Italian and German prisoners worked on the local farms along with Land Army girls. Some of these men married local women and remained in England after the war.

At Boddington, Iris Thomas explains that many women and children already helped out on local farms, so they were quite surprised one day to learn that they were going to be helped by German prisoners of war. The adults were worried by this but the children thought it was exciting. The Germans were brought under armed guard in a lorry and dropped off at different farms. Iris's farm received about ten POWs who worked really hard, thus helping to increase production. As time went by the children became friendly with them, especially the two who could speak a little English. Marcus was about 40 years old but Juke was only 19 and very homesick. They enjoyed practising their English and talked about their homes and families and how they never wanted to be in the army in the first place.

> One day at break time they brought out a small wooden animal which could be pulled along by a piece of string. They gave this toy to my young brother who was about three. We admired their craftsmanship and they asked us to collect old toothbrush handles which they then crafted into cigarette holders for us to give out as Christmas presents. They were very skilful and just wanted something to do back at the prison camp in the evenings. As time went by they became even more trusted and were not guarded by the army while at the farm. Eventually they must have moved camp and we were disappointed when they stopped coming.

At Tiverton in Devon, Geoff Grater was playing at the end of the road when someone tapped him on the shoulder. The man announced he was a German prisoner of war who had made an ashtray with a bird on it out of wood, and wanted £1 for it, or one hundred Players cigarettes. Geoff knew that his father had the necessary cigarettes and ran home to find out if he wanted to exchange them for this souvenir, but they were rationed so he refused to let Geoff have them, or buy the ashtray. He was also quite incensed by the fact that a prisoner could roam around the town at will. 'Who let him out' he wondered. 'They must need their head tested!'

At Testwood, where Italian POWs were employed on the maintenance of the canal and river Test, another prisoner showed his practical skill in making a signet ring for the sister of Anne Biffin. Although they wore special uniforms with large patches on them, she recalls that they appeared always to be laughing and singing. They loved to have children around and one of the men fashioned the signet ring from a silver threepenny piece. Local people were not supposed to fraternise with prisoners but nobody appeared to mind. Even though they were on strict rations, they would share their bread and cake with the local kids. 'There was just one German prisoner,' Anne reflects, 'and he kept himself apart from the Italians. We used to see him exercising the local farmer's hunter around the fields. He stayed on after the war, marrying a local girl.'

At Haverah Park, Italian prisoners were known to help out on a farm next to that of Molly Kinghorn's grandparents. Her Uncle George, whom she diplomatically describes as 'barking mad', chose to trade his clothes with one of them. She has no idea why he did this, as the Italians had no intention of escaping dressed as Englishmen, being 'too well looked after'. But he ended up sauntering around the locality with large diamond patches on his back and legs. The patches were to provide British soldiers with targets to aim at should they need to chase escaped prisoners. Uncle George must have thought they made him look a little dapper.

Other prisoners were found suitable employment within the community. At Holbeton in Devon, for instance the father of Jean Pearse, a First World War veteran and ARP warden, was also the village blacksmith. He was allocated a German prisoner to help him in the smithy. The man was called Philip and he told Jean that in Germany he had a daughter of about her age. He was 'such a nice man', she states, and she enjoyed taking him buns and cakes that her mother managed to bake with their rations.

50   *Children play near the walkway between the operating wards at the American army hospital in Axminster, built to receive casualties after D-Day. The photograph was taken shortly after the Americans had finally left, when the wards they built were converted into council accommodation.*

51   *A squadron of B-17s of the American 91st Bomb Group flying over East Anglia, taking the fight to the enemy on the continent. For children all over the counties of Suffolk and Norfolk, the huge formations crossing the coast line was a daily spectacle.*

Donald Patience clearly remembers German prisoners being billeted at Avoch on the Black Isle. Donald was a keen footballer whose position was in goal. On one occasion he played in a team against some of the prisoners. After attempting to punch the ball he collided with one of the German players, who fell to the floor in a heap with blood streaming from his ear. Donald panicked thinking he had killed the man, but his injury was not serious. These German footballers were perfect gentlemen, but he often wonders how his mother agreed to him playing against them in the first place, as he was only 15 years old at the time.

Late in the war there were both German and Italian prisoner of war camps around the outskirts of Bristol. The Germans were mainly deployed clearing up the damage caused by their own bombers, while the Italians seemed to be helping on the land. In the city, unlike the countryside, any kind of communication with these prisoners was strictly forbidden. There was however, one little game that Doreen Govan and her friends took part in as often as possible. If Italians were working on a bridge in the area, the sight of young girls on bikes would draw them to look over and wave. The trick Doreen explains, was to shout 'Balzac' at them and race under the bridge as fast as you could to avoid being pelted at the other side. 'To this day,' she admits, 'I have no idea why this particular word infuriated them, but it was a very amusing and rewarding exercise.'

Camp No. 57 was situated on Merrow Downs near the home of Audrey Purser in Surrey. Italian prisoners were the first to arrive here, followed later by the Germans. Audrey and the other children at school would hear them marching up and down the road in their heavy boots while they were in their classroom. In the winter, when it snowed, the Italians would make sledges for the local children. 'We would have great fun,' she states, 'going down the steep slope of the golf course. We only had trays to sit on, or perhaps a piece of wood with some runners underneath, but these did not go very fast. The sledges the Italians made could sit six children at once. The excitement and joy of speeding down the slopes combined with the fresh air meant we went home with rosy cheeks and smiles on our faces.'

Sometimes the children would creep up on to the Downs and the boys would dare each other to touch the fence around the camp where the Italians were incarcerated at night. Some of these lads would crawl up to the perimeter on their tummies, and when a guard saw them, they would spring up and take to their heels, along with all the other children observing from afar. In daylight hours the prisoners would play football, which would attract the children to the fence. The prisoners would wave and call to them in their own languages. Audrey recalls how the wonderful smell of bread being baked would drift towards them from the camp kitchens. It made them feel very hungry and prompted the journey home.

Towards the end of the war, German prisoners would march down the Epsom Road on their way to services at St John's church. The children would hear them singing as they swung their arms and thumped their heavy boots on the road

52 *Italian prisoners of war helping with the harvest on an English farm, watched over by an armed guard.*

surface. After the war Camp No. 57, along with many other similar camps and temporary wartime establishments, was taken over by Guildford Borough Council and turned into temporary accommodation for young families. Following the Blitz on major towns and cities, and the loss of so many homes, basic housing was needed for thousands of people.

Many of the prisoners chose to remain after the war, particularly the Italians. Several towns and cities have strong Italian communities that can trace their roots back to these turbulent times.

53   Safe in an English country garden. On Sunday afternoons during the war Pat Robinson and her family would go for walks around their home in Stroud. Sometimes they would meet Italian prisoners, also allowed out for walks, one of which was Gino who lived in Milan with his parents. They invited him home for tea and he subsequently became a friend of the family until he was later moved to Thornbury.

54   The smiles on their faces indicate that these Italian prisoners are happy their war is over. Two of them are seen in the background with a local child.

Chapter 5

Life on the Home Front

Almost everything the country produced, from food to clothes, was now needed by the armed forces if they were to win the day. Consequently everybody, from the youngest child to the most senior citizen, would experience rationing in its varied forms.

Food Rationing

It was not long after the start of the war that a system for rationing food was put in place. The German E-Boat threat made it more and more difficult to get supplies into British ports from other parts of the world so the food the nation consumed over the next few years would have to be almost entirely homegrown. To make sure everybody had an equal share of essential foodstuffs and to prevent shopkeepers benefitting from the shortages by raising prices, each person was limited to a restricted amount. On National Registration Day, 29 September 1939, every householder in the country was required to complete a form listing all those who lived at their address. Using this data the government issued everyone with their identity card and a ration book containing coupons. Then, from 8 January 1940, each time somebody wished to purchase a rationed item, they were required to hand their book to the retailer with the money, who would then either sign it, or cut out the necessary coupon.

A typical weekly supply of groceries was limited to four ounces of ham or bacon, two ounces of cheese, eight ounces of sugar, eight ounces of butter, margarine or lard, three pints of milk, two ounces of tea, four ounces of sweets, and one fresh egg per person. They could also have meat, other than bacon or ham, to the value of one shilling and twopence, which amounted roughly to four sausages and one pork chop. This quota does not seem to have been set in stone, and should be regarded as 'typical'. People quote different figures for the same items, and in different places at different times the amounts seem to vary. The system was intended to be fair but made allowance for children. Marie Litchfield notes that it was 'carefully planned so that small children were entitled to extra body-building foodstuffs'.

Ration books were colour coded and there were three varieties: those under five had a green one, while for older children it was blue and for adults buff. Marie explains that:

> This assured, as far as possible, that the nation's growing children were provided with at least the basic provisions for healthy growth. On the green ration book, could be obtained a regular supply of cod-liver oil – hated by all, but very good for you. Concentrated orange juice was also available on these books,

*55   Cover of ration
book issued to
Roy Stevens from
Broadstone in Dorset.*

for the price of a postage stamp. It was a valuable source of vitamin C, and much more pleasant. Sometimes, when a certain food was in short supply, a notice would go up in the shop window: 'Only on green ration books,' so that the little ones would not be deprived; and everyone understood and respected this. Powdered milk, dried eggs, margarine instead of butter – these were facts of living.

At Cayton, Jenny Peacock also recalls the joys of cod-liver oil taken with orange juice to compensate for the vitamins missing from diets. 'It wouldn't have been so bad,' she explains, 'but mother insisted on a big spoonful of cod-liver oil first. I can still remember the thick oil going slowly down my throat and the strong fishy taste, followed by a good spoonful of the sour orange juice. These induced in me a horrible sick feeling.' However, she notes that most of the generation who were war children have good strong bones and thick, shiny hair today. Another substance forced on the nation's children, was Virol with malt extract but Mrs Peacock admits to having quite liked this because it resembled a soft toffee in a jar. She goes on to suggest that children had better food to eat during rationing than they often do today.

Not everything was rationed and, in particular, locally grown seasonal fruit and vegetables could be consumed at will. Of course, this was slightly unfair on people living in cities as these items were not as easily obtainable as they were to those living in the country. Similarly, country people found it easier to obtain fresh eggs; for those in town, limited to their one fresh egg a week, something called dried egg was introduced in a powdered form which had to be mixed with water. Doreen Govan remembers omelettes made from this substance which 'had the texture of leather'. For babies, dried milk became available.

Fish and chips, very popular at the time, were not rationed but, due to the continued E-Boat attacks it became increasingly difficult to supply fresh fish direct from the North Sea, while tinned fish from foreign canneries was unobtainable. Doreen Govan recalls 'a simply filthy item called dried

56   Lunch for children at a Battersea feeding centre is made memorable by the presence of the King and Queen.

Atlantic Cod, great slabs of the saltiest dried fish imaginable, which had to be soaked for days before being ready to cook and eat. Not worth the effort.' Potatoes on the other hand were the nation's staple diet and were served to children in many ways. At Ammanford, Myra Williams had potatoes at many a meal. Large potatoes would be washed and put in the oven to cook all day. Particularly large ones would have a cross cut in them, into which butter or margarine would be forced. 'We'd eat it all,' she says. 'The skin was crisp and good for us.'

You could not take your ration book to the store of your fancy but you had to register with particular shops and use your coupons on their premises. In Devizes, for instance, Bill Underwood's uncle and auntie had a small grocery shop, so his parents chose to register with them. Whether or not the system was fair rather depended on where you lived and who your supplier was. Doreen Govan explains that if your grocer was a 'good un', as Mr Cook was in Bristol, he would save up a few scarce extras until he had enough for all his customers, ensuring that there was an equal, if somewhat small, amount for each. This was all part of the wartime spirit and was known as 'under

57   *An apple a day! Children under five went to the front of a queue, with first choice of any oranges or other available fruit, together with a daily pint of milk and a double supply of eggs.*

the counter'. However, the system could be abused, and Roy Stevens remembers that at Broadstone, where he was sent to collect the family meat ration, the local butcher produced 'under the counter' packages for favoured customers. 'He was a formidable character,' says Roy, 'so nobody dared to complain.' However, a green ration book usually led pregnant women, nursing mothers and children under five to the front of a queue, with first choice of any oranges or other available fruit, together with a daily pint of milk and a double supply of eggs. Children between five and sixteen with blue ration books were allowed fruit, the full meat ration and half a pint of milk daily.

The Ministry of Food tried to encourage people to eat healthily, distributing recipes printed on yellow slips of paper. Perhaps the best known of these was Woolton Pie, named after the Food Minister, Lord Woolton. Doreen Govan notes that 'this consisted of mixed vegetables with a few soaked dried peas, moistened with an Oxo cube and topped with mashed potato'. Bill Underwood also tasted Woolton Pie, but his favourite wartime dishes included 'milk sops for breakfast, which were pieces of bread warmed up in milk.' He also had a liking for fried bread and jam. At Cayton, Jenny Peacock was fed on what her mother called bread bailie, which consisted of bread softened with warm milk and a few raisins thrown in. 'I still can't look at bread and butter pudding even now,' she squirms. And in Merrow Audrey Purser's mother would fill them up with one of her 'wonderful bacon puddings'. This had bacon and chopped onions rolled up in flour and suet, then tied with a piece of cloth and boiled for hours. It was served with a few vegetables grown in the garden.

Some families coped more easily with rationing than others. Marie Litchfield, for instance, recalls that it wasn't really that much of a hardship for her family because they were already accustomed to living frugally. Her mother was clever at managing and at making nourishing meals out of unpromising provisions. 'She was before her time in realising the value of pulses, and potatoes were usually available at a reasonable price,' she writes, 'after the delicious, home-grown "first earlies" were finished. We were well content with a baked potato for our dinner.' Sweets were understandably rationed but Marie was not that bothered: 'We hardly ever bought sweets,' she admits, 'so could give away our sweet coupons.' In Weston-super-Mare, Margaret Cable explains that her mother would save up their sweet coupons in order to have lots on special occasions. One Christmas her mother came back from the shop proudly clutching a dozen 2oz bars of chocolate. Margaret suggests, 'She must have been saving for months.'

Betty Howat was a pupil at Worcester Grammar School for Girls and describes some of the recipes that were introduced in the face of rationing:

> I remember we made potato cakes, and one week we made blancmange using cornflour. We were shown how to prepare dried egg, and dried banana. Bananas and oranges were in short supply because we could not import them. It was not easy to get ingredients for children to practise with. We were also taught about the working of the gas stove and how to wash a tea towel by hand.

So throughout the war years, children lived on a strict but ultimately quite healthy diet, especially when compared to the way people eat in modern Britain. And even after the war had finished, it took quite a while for the food industry to recover properly. Food rationing in Britain only ended at midnight on 4 July 1954, when restrictions on the sale and purchase of meat and bacon were lifted, nine years after the end of the war.

58   *Hazel Reigate is standing at the left of this photograph, with other members of the Croydon junior detachment of the British Red Cross Society. It was taken in a large basement restaurant, and the food was provided by local shop owners to cheer up 'deprived children in war-torn Croydon,' whose schools had been closed by air raids.*

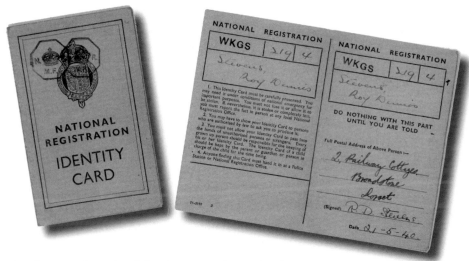

59   *Cover and inside of the identity card issued to Roy Stevens, who was five when the war began.*

As well as their ration books, children were also issued with their identity cards and Molly Kinghorn explains that your number became imprinted on your mind, hers being KRNO 8 4. Similarly, Doreen Govan remembers her number, OANC 162 3, while Elizabeth Gillett from Brighton describes having to wear an identity disc. Those who could afford them had bracelets, but because her family were poor they were provided with a free disc on a piece of string, which they hung around the neck. Colin Russell, who lived in the village of Fradley in Staffordshire, explains how identification numbers worked. The area code for Fradley was OTLN and each family in the village was given a number, theirs being 65. Then, each member of the family had a number according to status. The senior member, usually the father, would be number 1, mother 2, eldest child 3, and so on. So Colin's number, as an eldest child, was OTLN 65 3.

Dig for Victory

Every family with access to a garden or allotment was encouraged to grow as much of their own food as possible. As Marie Litchfield points out, 'Everything that could be grown at home saved valuable ships, manpower, time and money. The nation had to be kept fed and healthy with the minimum of imported foodstuffs. "Dig for Victory" was one of the many slogans of the day, and people set to with a will to grow all they could. Patches of hitherto unused ground were dug and planted, and many a flower bed was turned into a vegetable plot.'

In Leeds, Molly Kinghorn also remembers the call to 'Dig for Victory'. Their house was close to Cross Flatts Park, and she recalls that the grassy areas were deemed suitable for allotments. Her father applied for one of these and was successful. Then came the mammoth task of removing all the grass. To encourage them to help him, her father agreed to let his children keep anything they found whilst preparing his allotment. 'My sister and I soon had a hoard of things,' notes Molly, 'combs, penknives, hair clips, pennies and sixpences. I think Dad regretted it when I found half a crown, a little fortune in those days.' The main crops on the allotments were potatoes, peas, beans, cabbages and sprouts, although Molly's father also grew cucumbers. One thing that aggravated her father, she recalls, was the man on the next allotment, whom he described as coming 'three sheets in the wind' and planting everything all over the place. But despite this he produced magnificent crops. 'My Dad had the last laugh,' claims Molly, 'when some bombs were dropped right down the middle of the park and all his plants were scattered far and wide, some ending up on the roof of our house. We were very lucky as most of our allotment was undamaged. Two young boys fire watching ran down the street with stones, soil and various vegetables bouncing off their tin hats.'

Many schools that had gardens, especially in rural areas, took part in the 'Back to the Land' campaign, in which children grew large quantities of vegetables as part of the regular curriculum. At Eastrington in the East Riding of Yorkshire, Doreen Wilde (née White) attended the grammar school at nearby Goole, and occasionally her entire class would help a local farmer 'take up potatoes', as part of the war effort. And in the village of Llanhrian in Pembrokeshire, Mr Charles remembers the farmers would visit the school and ask for volunteers for both potato planting and picking, as well as helping with the harvest. The headmaster would allow any children who were over the age of 13 to volunteer.

Groups of girls from Stroud High School, including Pat Robinson who lived in the Dudbridge Hill area of the town, were occasionally taken by lorry to go potato planting at Slimbridge. When they arrived the potato fields seemed to stretch almost to infinity. The girls were shown what to do and, most importantly, instructed to have nothing to do with the Italian prisoners who were also working there. There was little chance of this anyway, as the prisoners worked in the dim distance.

60 *School children participating in the 'Back to the land' campaign. Working on the school garden in Kent as part of the regular curriculum.*

Doreen Wilde's house had a pantry, two steps lower than the kitchen. Nobody in those days had freezers or fridges, but things kept cool in the pantry, including milk which the children would fetch in a tin can from Mr Brown the farmer. Doreen remembers that when they fetched the milk it was often still warm. In Cayton, the father of Jenny Peacock worked on a local farm so was able to bring home fresh milk straight from the cow. She notes how 'many a child caught a TB germ from the milk and ended up with large scars down their neck that had to be lanced'.

Some people also provided their own meat. The family of Doreen Wilde kept pigs and were allowed to kill two a year. The local butcher came to the house to slaughter it and the ham and bacon was covered in salt and left for a few weeks until it was 'cured'. Doreen's mother had a mincer fixed to a wooden table and some of the meat was cut up and minced to make sausages. At Ammanford, Myra Williams recalls that many households kept both chickens and pigs. All left-over scraps would be boiled to make pig swill. Some families would buy a cockerel, goose or duck, to fatten up for Christmas dinner, and these would be fed with household scraps and boiled potato peelings.

61 *Digging for victory. The Queen visits an evacuation school in Horsted Keynes, where a boy from Battersea helps prepare ground for food crops.*

Doreen Wilde and her two brothers joined the local rabbit club, which meant they were permitted a ration of feed from the village shop for each animal, as long as they were reared for consumption. They would also glean corn from their father's fields, and collect dandelions and other greens. The rabbits were eventually sold to a local butcher who took them to Hull market. Frank Hind's mother kept some two hundred rabbits in a range of hutches on their farm. These kept the family in both meat and furs, and she also took them to rabbit shows, often winning prizes. Jenny Peacock describes how her mother had the ability to skin a rabbit completely with two swift tugs. Being squeamish, she vacated the kitchen at such times, although hunger would get the better of her once it was cooked. Occasionally the local butcher would swap around fifteen rabbits for one bit of shoulder of beef.

There were other ways of obtaining meat. Although the father of Donald Patience was a fisherman at Avoch, able to supply a limited amount of fresh fish, Donald admits that as a youngster he would often poach a rabbit or two for his mother's pot. Having moved from Norwich to the rural town of Wymondham, Ron Green would often poach a partridge on his way home from school. Having located a nest, he had the choice of either taking the eggs or, with a swift glance

62   *Frank Hind (right) and his brother, with one of the two hundred or so rabbits reared by their mother which kept the family in meat and furs.*

from a hazel stick, taking the partridge itself. If the partridge was sitting on a full nest of eggs it wouldn't budge, he claims, and was therefore easy to approach. Ron was just one of many people doing this until, eventually, posters on trees offered a £200 reward for information about anyone taking game. 'Still I often came home looking like a buxom wench,' he admits.

For those living in the countryside, nature itself provided stocks for the larder and children relished the chance to help their mothers replenish these. Marie Litchfield notes that children and adults scoured the woods and hedgerows for wild fruits. 'Blackberries, rosehips, crab-apples, elderberries, sloes – everything that could be eaten was eagerly gathered in,' she recalls. Some of these would be turned into jam, syrup, chutney or just simply bottled for the lean days of winter. Frank Hind would drive up to the Quantock Hills with his mother in their pony and trap to pick whortleberries. At Avoch, Donald Patience had fun picking wild raspberries to make jam, and blackberries to make bramble and apple jelly. At Amberley in West Sussex, Pamela Gear's school class was taken to Arundel Park to pick deadly nightshade, which she believes was used medicinally. In Herefordshire, Margaret Wilce would pick chestnuts and beechnuts in the autumn, while in the spring they gathered hawthorn leaves, which they called 'bread and cheese'. On the way home from school, she and her friends were not averse to 'scrumping' a local farmer's pears and cider apples, which she admits had a very sour taste. But the blackberries they picked would be bought by a local man who came round the cottages with a lorry. He weighed them and you were paid accordingly. They tried to make enough money out of this trade to buy winter shoes, although her arms and legs were always sore from bramble scratches.

Where possible, people would share their excess food with other families. Doreen Wilde remembers how sausages made from their pig were shared with neighbours, who in turn shared theirs with them when their pigs were killed. Jenny Peacock notes that a lot of 'swapping went on'. She believes ration books lasted about a month at a time, and if you ran out of a particular coupon you either did without or tried your hand at bartering. Sugar was the most common currency and could be swapped for most things. Audrey Purser remembers that, 'When one person had something which another person wanted, they would do a swap. There was a good community spirit in Down Road and that was to last for many years.'

Later in the war, after the Americans arrived and the E-Boat threat had been virtually eliminated, things began to improve. Doreen Govan explains how they received parcels from America and were introduced to previously unknown delicacies, such as spam and peanut butter. Margaret Harber in Swindon had Australian relatives that would send her 'wonderful food parcels'. These contained items that were unobtainable in Britain and she fondly remembers rich fruitcakes baked and sent in the same tin.

Make Do and Mend

Many other things became scarce during the war because industry was dedicated to providing things for the war effort. If any rare item became available people were prepared to queue for hours. Doreen Govan remembers how she and her mother would queue up to buy cigarettes for her father. 'You had to queue for everything in those days,' she recalls, 'and the longer the war went on the scarcer things became.' Queues became noticeably longer and it got to the stage that 'if you saw a queue, you joined it, regardless of what was being sold, or whether you wanted it or not'. At the end of the day, whatever scarce item you had bought was something to barter with for things you did need. At Gravesend in Kent, Julie Baker says that if a luxury item such as nylon stockings were known to be in a particular store and her mother could not get there, she would send Julie and her brother to queue up with the ration books. Her mother worked in a local solicitor's office, and the children would keep her place until she was able to get there herself after work as the retailers would not sell such items directly to children.

Clothes and other items made from material were rationed from 1 June 1941 until 15 March 1949 because clothing factories and people who normally worked in the rag trade were busy making items for the war effort such as uniforms, parachutes and balloons. People were also urged to 'Make do and mend'. The government issued everyone with a Clothing Book that contained coloured coupons. There were no coupons for particular items, but each piece of clothing had a value in points. When purchasing clothes the buyer handed the shopkeeper the money and Clothing Book and the retailer would cut out coupons which equated to the item's value. This system allowed people to buy approximately one completely new set of clothes a year.

The coupons were coloured in order to stop people using them all at once. Initially the books contained 60 coupons, which if you observed the colours would last a year, but this was later reduced to forty-eight. If you ran out of one colour, you waited until the government said it was time to begin using the next. If you had not used up all of the first

63 *Julie Baker, at five, pictured on the roof of her school gym in Gravesend in 1940, wearing an 'Irish dancing outfit'. Her mother made her and her brother queue up for things in shops, keeping a place until she could go.*

64 *This photograph of Pat Robinson (left) and her friends on the steps of Stroud High School, is a good study of the style of dresses that teenage girls wore both in and out of the classroom in the 1940s.*

colour by that time, you were allowed to carry the coupons forward to the next period. Children were allocated an extra ten clothing coupons, in case they grew out of their clothes during the year. Coupons had also to be used to buy school clothes, and if you went to a school that demanded you wear a particular uniform, such as Worcester Grammar School for Girls attended by Betty Howat, this piled added pressure on to parents. Betty explains that, 'All clothes were on coupons including school uniform: grey cotton dresses, Panama hats and blazers in the summer, and pleated navy skirts, red jumpers, heavy top coats and felt hats for winter.'

At Tasburgh, in Norfolk William Moore recalls that items like sheets, pillowcases, blankets and tea towels were also purchased through the coupon system. Schoolboys, he explains, would normally have three pairs of trousers, one short pair for school, one pair for Sunday best, and one pair for playing in. If you were of a nervous disposition and wetted your trousers during the day, there were no spares to put on and no time to wash and dry them, so your mother simply dried them out by the fireside over night. This often led to embarrassment the next day because body heat and room temperature caused the dried urine to whiff a bit. 'Girls were in a better situation,' he claims, 'as knickers were easily and readily changed.' He goes on to explain that 'My personal humiliation was having to wear cut down thick black nurses stockings when I had no socks.' In those days socks were made from wool, and almost all available wool was used for the manufacture of uniforms. It became very scarce and purchasing it meant going without something else. Clothing coupons, he states, 'had to be used very thoughtfully, as the scarcer the item, the more coupons one had to hand over.'

If you were prepared to make your own garments, buying cloth from a roll was cheaper than manufactured goods. So mothers who could sew, knit and use a sewing machine had an advantage over other women. But, as the war went on new clothes became increasingly scarce, so 'make do and mend' became a way of life. Jenny Peacock, for instance, had a coat made from army blankets. To make it look nice her mother put red piping around the edges and sewed red buttons down the front. However, it was not very warm and one cold winter's day, when she went across the fields to play with her brothers, she nearly froze to death when snow fell 'by the bucket full'. Unable to get home she ended up with hypothermia. The doctor laid her out in front of the range in the kitchen, where she thawed out and soon bounced back to full health.

When wool was available, mothers, grandmothers and aunties would also do a lot of knitting. They would often make balaclava helmets for the children, the snugness of the fit depending on the skill of the knitter. Mrs Peacock remembers having 'one lovely little knitted dress' which was sent to her by an uncle serving in the RAF and stationed in the Azores.

Doreen Govan recalls that the clothes situation was particularly bad for growing children, as all their clothes had to be worn until they fell apart. Then they were unpicked and the best parts made into something else. She goes on to explain that:

> The government kept giving out slogans for us. 'Make do and mend' meant exactly that and 'patches are patriotic' became the norm. Most mothers became quite accomplished at this job, because clothes were mostly made at home, anyway. Mothers were adept at knitting and sewing so bought clothes were considered very second rate, except for thick winter coats, which were a necessity.

65 *Jenny Peacock wearing the knitted dress sent to her from the Azores by an uncle serving in the RAF.*

Doreen Wilde also recalls how old jumpers were unpicked and the wool rescued to make something else. Boys wore boots, never shoes, for school and had studs in them to make the leather last longer. 'We had a village cobbler who mended shoes and boots,' she says and you 'had to be careful with clothes because often they were a lot of coupons to replace'.

Marie Litchfield's mother was also good at sewing, her own mother having been a trained and highly skilled dressmaker.

> Mother didn't pretend to be an expert, but she could cut down old jackets and trousers and make children's wear from them; she also turned things inside out and made them up on the other side. One of the wartime slogans was 'make do and mend' and she certainly fulfilled this injunction to the letter. She was helped by gifts of passed-on clothing. Father had friends from his Cambridge days who still kept in touch; they had children a little older than we were, who went to boarding school and had very good clothes. Their parcels arrived at our house now and again and were always hailed with glee by Bou and me, and no doubt with a certain relief by mother.

Because of this ability to clothe the family, Marie's family's own clothing coupons were sometimes passed on to other people.

The mother of Margaret Wilce also coped admirably with the situation and would spend many winter evenings, knitting, sewing or crocheting. She would make most of Margaret's clothes, unstitching a navy coat that belonged to her

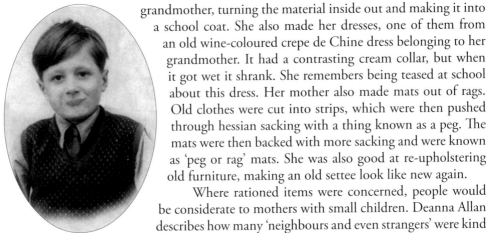

66   *This photograph of David Andrews shows some of the typical clothes worn by a young lad during the war years.*

grandmother, turning the material inside out and making it into a school coat. She also made her dresses, one of them from an old wine-coloured crepe de Chine dress belonging to her grandmother. It had a contrasting cream collar, but when it got wet it shrank. She remembers being teased at school about this dress. Her mother also made mats out of rags. Old clothes were cut into strips, which were then pushed through hessian sacking with a thing known as a peg. The mats were then backed with more sacking and were known as 'peg or rag' mats. She was also good at re-upholstering old furniture, making an old settee look like new again.

Where rationed items were concerned, people would be considerate to mothers with small children. Deanna Allan describes how many 'neighbours and even strangers' were kind to her family of girls. 'The elderly would bring little extra rations to the door,' she notes. She also relates the story of a bus trip to Stamford with her mother and grandmother whilst her two sisters were at school. Her mother spotted a good pair of secondhand shoes in the market and asked the stallholder what price they were. She was hoping to use her bargaining skills as money was always tight. 'Is your man serving?' the woman asked. After being told that the husband was away in the Royal Navy, she smiled and handed her the shoes, saying 'Well you have them Love, and good luck to you my dear.' It was a tale of wartime kindness that Deanna's mother liked to retell years after the event.

Later in the war the Red Cross opened exchange centres for children's clothing, which again worked on a system of points. Marie Litchfield recalls these centres:

> You took in some of your own children's clothes, providing they were in good condition, and were awarded so many points for each garment. With these you could acquire other clothes, according to your present needs. Sometimes there were new garments, like jumpers, and other hand-knitted items that had been made by schoolchildren and various other well-wishers for distribution by the Red Cross. A lot of these had been made in the USA to send to children in war-torn countries. One little dress that Mother brought back for Bridget had a note pinned inside the pocket from a schoolgirl in America, addressed to 'the little English girl who gets this dress'. Bridget herself wasn't old enough to write back, but one of the family did, because the address was on the note. A few letters were exchanged, but the correspondence fizzled out after a while.

Doing Their Bit for the War Effort

As the shortage of metal to manufacture bombs and other munitions became more acute, the government began to take extreme measures to obtain it. In Somerset, Marie Litchfield remembers the day when a notice went up on the village green notice board stating that all iron fences, gates and railings were required for making munitions, and would be removed. 'We were very anxious,' she ponders, 'because though we only had one little iron gate, at the end of the front path, it opened

67 Doreen Wilde pictured as a bridesmaid in Beverley Minster in 1939, when she was six.

onto a flight of five steep steps down onto the road.' Her family feared that if there was no gate, a toddler, such as her baby sister, could be down those steps before anyone could stop them. 'We hoped those concerned with the collection would appreciate our dilemma,' she notes, but they didn't. 'A big lorry came round the village, and the man took everyone's gate off its hinges and removed it, to make bombs. Our little gate went, too, and though most people in time made or bought wooden ones, we couldn't afford one. However, no one ever did fall down the steps.'

As time went on, the government found new ways to raise money for weapons, and often children were able to help out and 'do their bit'. As Marie Litchfield and her sister Bou grew older and entered their early teens, they began to take what they considered a more active part in the war effort. They had already been helping on the domestic side with the growing and gathering of crops and wild fruit, but new initiatives to raise funds for the armed forces were in place. Marie remembers:

> Events were organised all over the country and everyone was asked to cooperate where and as they could. Some of the cities and towns put on ambitious ventures. People rose to the challenge and a lot of talent emerged. Songs were written, entertainments of various kinds produced, and imaginative ways thought out for getting cash. The villages hadn't as much to draw on in the way of expertise or wherewithal but had easily as much keenness and enthusiasm.

There were three big fund-raising drives over the years called 'Salute the Soldier Week', 'Warship Week', and 'Wings for Victory', devised to raise money for each of the armed forces in turn. At Eastrington, Doreen Wilde recalls the various 'War Weeks' and people being encouraged to buy savings certificates known as war bonds. 'Each village and town tried to raise as much money as possible,' she states. Margaret Wilce was encouraged to take sixpence weekly to school to buy Saving Stamps that would eventually purchase a Savings Certificate for fifteen shillings. Bill Underwood remembers 'War Weapons Week' during the month of May 1941, when, all the local schools were asked to enter their pupils in a

68 Members of the Junior Red Cross knitting bedsocks and other comforts for wounded soldiers, at Corporation Road Girls' School, in Newport, Monmouthshire.

poster competition. 'My poster was selected as the best in the school,' he proudly claims. It was exhibited in one of the windows in a large department store and portrayed a line of Nazi stormtroopers goose stepping with rifles: its caption was 'Save your money to buy guns and we will beat these murderous Huns.'

People would do all manner of wonderful things to raise money for the forces. At Ammanford, the children at school with Myra Williams were asked to bring old saucepans which could be melted down to make aircraft. Every September they would go around the local farms and houses to collect money for a Spitfire. Roy Stevens remembers his school sending the older pupils out in pairs with a wheelbarrow to collect waste paper from local residents. These were called 'Waste Paper Drives' and, according to Roy, as well as doing some public good they were a nice way of skipping lessons!

The event that affected Marie Litchfield's own family most was the Bring and Buy sale, which involved most of the village in some capacity. Although many younger men and women were away in the forces, there was usually a dance in the village hall with music being provided by a piano or small band. School children put on sketches and songs, with an adult occasionally taking part as conjurer or ventriloquist. You brought anything you wanted to get rid of or could spare in the way of household goods or bric-a-brac. Some made things especially for the occasion. Certain housewives even managed, despite the meagre rations, to make and bring home cooking, which was snapped up at once. Many were the recipes that the enterprising cooks thought up for cakes without eggs, sometimes even without fat, and with the minimum of sugar. Marie describes the effort that went into these events.

> Bou and I worked hard beforehand with our needles and bits of material scrounged from other people's rag-bags. Any kind of soft toy sold well, and lavender bags, and babies' bibs. We had a little stall of our own, and stood behind it when the great afternoon came, proudly selling our wares, and feeling we had done so much for the war effort when we came to hand in our takings. Well, we had. And often we didn't even have the penny or twopence required to buy ourselves a cup of tea or a little bun. It was hard work, but it was all fun, and that I think was one of the main fruits of those 'weeks'. I suppose a lot of money was raised, but that would have soon been spent. Of more lasting value was the working together towards a goal (every area had its own target) and the enjoyment of everyone who participated. Friendships were forged, people felt good, and made others feel good.

On one occasion an elderly lady who lived alone had nothing to give to the Bring and Buy but wanting to contribute something as she was very patriotic, she went into her garden, cut her entire patch of hyacinths and put them in a pail of water. But because people were on the lookout for necessities like edible goods, clothing and gifts, rather than the luxury of cut flowers, nobody bought them. Marie and Bou went home and told their father, who did not usually attend such events himself. He had no cash but sent the girls back to get them, promising to send the money later. When they returned, though, Marie found that the flowers had already gone.

We hurried to the lady's house, and found that someone else had had the same feelings and hurried back to buy them after all. I tell this reminiscence because it highlights the spirit of concern and sensitivity of so many ordinary people living together through a time of so much trial and uncertainty. In spite of the harshness, the brutality, the senselessness of war, there remained a delicacy of touch in human nature that could not be fractured.

With the majority of men doing military service, and women working in the factories and fields, many children were able to 'do their bit' by undertaking various forms of war work. They might help on farms or allotments, or pack parcels for the Red Cross. Doreen Govan remembers that in Bristol many children helped fill sandbags that were then placed around historic or important buildings in order to protect them. At Axmouth, June Richards states 'We all took part in war work no matter how young we were.' She remembers night after night knitting things like string vests, pullovers and socks 'for the boys'. She would also help the lady across the road, known as 'Granny Rice,' mend mosquito nets for the troops based in warmer climates. She recalls spreading the massive cream nets over a dark wood table, to find any runs in them that needed to be sewn up. As June received a small amount of pocket money for this, she considers it to have been her very first paid job. And in Leeds, Molly Kinghorn remembers knitting socks for soldiers as well as scarves out of khaki wool. Old jumpers would be unstitched and the wool reused to fashion mittens and gloves.

As well as doing their bit for the war effort, children in the 1940s, were expected to do a lot more around the house. In Norfolk, Ron Green explains that most of the children had plenty of chores to do. Each day before school they went to the village well with buckets to fetch mother's water for the day. Other jobs might include digging a row of potatoes, cleaning the oil lamps, emptying the 'po' bucket, feeding the chickens and rabbits, fetching fire wood, or chopping some kindling. Some had miles to walk or cycle in all weathers, but Ron recalls how late arrivals would

69   *A party of school children helping to gather and bag potatoes on a farm in Surrey.*

70   *Many women and children helped out on local farms. This would often bring them into contact with Land Army girls, or prisoners of war, many of whom were also employed in agriculture.*

be locked out of school and expected to line up outside the assembly hall, which rang with the singing of classmates. Some of these children, he explains, had been helping their mothers since around 6.30am, but now they were marched in front of the school to make their excuses. 'Got a puncture miss, was one excuse,' he recalls. 'However, a stroke of the cane would be the next thing you'd get.'

Once when Ron was starting out for school his mother was not feeling very well, so she asked him to tell the lady over the lane to come over and visit her. Ron did so and set off for school. But, he admits his route often caused him to dilly dally, as there was an American army dump along the way where he would search for spent cartridges or comics. He could also be sidetracked by nesting birds. He was late again and locked out of the hall, joining the others as they stepped on to the stage to receive their punishment. After their caning, 'some would face the whole school and do a bow to cheers and laughter,' he recalls, 'but would then be called back by the headmistress for a double dose.' It then came to his turn. 'When the cane comes down,' he informs us, 'if you lower your hand at the right moment it hardly hurt.' But this time the headmistress held his wrist and then, to his amazement raised it high above his head proclaiming, 'This boy is a hero, a credit to the whole school. He saved his mother's life this morning when she fell down a well.' The message, that had arrived before him had somehow got mixed up as it was passed. 'Now what was I to do?' he deliberates, 'tell the head teacher that she'd got it all wrong and make her feel a fool in front of the whole school?' Ron quickly decided to say nothing and remain a hero for the day.

In time, Ron got wise to the fact that the actual roll call was not done until you were sitting in your classes, so if you were late it was better to sneak into class after assembly, rather than line up outside the hall. This way you might not be noticed.

71   *Certificate presented to whoever 'Has helped to provide comfort and contentment to the soldiers, sailors and airmen of the British Commonwealth.'*

Chapter 6

A Time for Play

Although children helped more around the home, 'did their bit' for the war effort, and were expected to act more responsibly at an earlier age, they were still children after all and needed 'a time for play'.

Toys and Games

Like many things, toys and children's games were considered non-essential and the factories that manufactured them were more likely to be making parts for real aircraft and fighting vehicles, than toy ones. New toys virtually disappeared from shops, and before long even the toy shops themselves disappeared, their premises being used for other purposes.

Frank Stanford was very keen on Meccano and before the war his combined wage as telegram boy, grocery boy and golf caddy was saved in a moneybox towards this hobby. At the start of the war the golf course was closed down to make way for railway lines carrying giant guns to the coast to fire shells at France. But this still left the money he earned in his other jobs, as well as any pocket money he might gather along the way. 'At the start of the war I went down to Dover by bus,' he recalls, 'to buy more Meccano parts.' He had a pound saved up, and Curry's sold the item in question. The shop was fifteen minutes walk from the main bus station and Frank was inside when there was a loud explosion somewhere in the town centre. 'The manager made me get under the counter with him,' he explains. 'Within a few minutes there were more giant explosions. The shop window came away and fell on the pavement, breaking up, and all the contents of the window were blown over the pavement and road.' The town was being subjected to a shelling from German guns across the Channel in France. After an hour in the shop, Frank eventually left with his Meccano. The shop manager was sweeping up broken glass and picking up items that had been blown out of his window. When Frank arrived back at the bus station it was gone and the area was pitted with craters. He recalls seeing destroyed shops, including one called Luptons, which he remembers vividly because its sign was lying in one of the craters. There were dead bodies and body parts everywhere. 'As a twelve year old, viewing all of this made me very sick,' he says. 'Ambulances and fire engines arrived. So I had to walk home. I found out later the main bus station had been hit with three shells that day. Fifty people were killed and many injured. In total Dover had 4,000 shells land on it, and 148 people killed, no wonder it was called Hell Fire Corner.'

It was thanks to bomb damage that, in Suffolk, a young Joy Matthews was able to acquire additions to the contents of her doll's house. A friend of her neighbour owned a toy shop in Diss which was damaged by bomb blast, so one day she asked Joy's mother if she would be interested in purchasing toys that had to be cleared. Most of them were made in Germany or Japan and had been stored in the attic of the shop for the duration of the war, because they were regarded as unpatriotic. The bomb-damaged attic had now to be cleared. Joy explains that:

> I was about four and was collecting little things for my doll's house. I was absolutely delighted to see so many miniature objects and of course I wanted them all. Money was tight and my Mother had just grabbed her change purse when we came out, so in the end I had to make a choice. I picked a white tea set with pink flowers on it, two glass candelabra, some pictures in gilt frames, felt flowers in rubber flower pots, a glass tumbler, a black stick telephone and a wonderful cocktail glass with a blue and green swirly stem. I dearly wanted a tiny baby doll which at two shillings, would have gone over the budget, so I had to be content with these items. We spent around ten shillings which was probably all the housekeeping my Mother had left. I still have the sugar bowl from the tea set and the glass tumbler. And I have since bought the baby doll at an antique fair and believe me it cost more than ten new pence.

Most families in the 1930s could not afford to buy their children many toys, and favourite toys were often home-made and improvised. In Devizes, Bill Underwood and his mates constructed go-karts from pram wheels, planks of wood and thick string, which was used for steering the front wheels. In these ramshackle death-traps, the children would hurtle down the hill towards the railway station. On one occasion, Bill was standing on the back of a cart while his friend John

72   *Germany was no longer able to dominate the world toy market as it had traditionally done and British exports increased dramatically. Model aeroplanes were a popular line, although many of the factories making toys would soon be employed making things for the war effort.*

73 *Looking through the window of a 1930s toy shop. Toys virtually disappeared from shops, and before long even the shops themselves had disappeared, their premises being used for other purposes.*

Wintermere did the steering. When they neared the bottom of the hill, while going at some speed, they noticed a gentleman called Bob Tanner stepping out to cross the road and loaded with the evening papers he was going to sell. With no brakes it was impossible to stop, so Bill quickly jumped off, but the go-kart, with John steering it, smashed straight into Bob. The man was laid out semi conscious while poor John kept saying 'Sorry Mr Tanner, sorry Mr Tanner.' The boys scurried away leaving a crowd of people gathered around. The following evening Bill was helping his father in his barber's shop when Mr Tanner walked in to deliver the evening paper. Bill noticed that he had a black eye and several grazes on his face. His father asked, 'What happened to you Bob?' and the man replied 'Some little buggers knocked me down at the station.' Bill kept quiet and believes that neither his father nor Mr Tanner realised for some time that he was one of the culprits.

There was a variety of other toys available for children. Marie Litchfield's brother Simon had a toy farm, and little lead models of animals, fences, waggons and farmer, all made perfectly to scale, and he played with them endlessly, especially on dreary wet days. Marie thinks her parents bought the collection, one piece at a time, over many years. Other boys collected lead soldiers. Geoff Grater, who grew up in Tiverton, remembers children having a very healthy life style, always playing out of doors. He made bows and arrows to play 'Cowboys and Indians', and acorn pipes by hollowing out an acorn and putting a straw in it to suck through. They also had peashooters and catapults, which he admits were a bit dangerous. Children would roam over fields, much to the annoyance of the farmers or go fishing in local streams for sticklebacks which would be carried home in jam jars. Occasionally they caught lizards and slow worms. Less healthily, though, Geoff and his friends were always searching for 'dog ends to smoke' which adults had thrown away. Sometimes they even made cigarettes themselves from used tea leaves. 'So we grew up healthy,' he emphasises, 'running about and not having excess food to eat. We did not suffer from obesity like kids today'.

At Catford in south east London, Alan Kerry and his friends played in roads which were empty of cars. They did not have a real football so used a tin with a few stones in it to kick around. Alan also had a bicycle wheel and a short stick, and would run down the street with the wheel at his side. His friends would tie a long piece of string from one knocker to another, so when one person opened their door, it would knock the other one. Of course, the boys were nowhere to be seen. In London among the bomb sites, children enjoyed playing out of doors for hours on end:

> At one time I would walk from Catford to Black Heath. I can remember Black Heath, a very large park land, with a large pond. Other kids and I would go fishing there. If we had no money for nets, then we would use sacks. Sometimes we got something, other times not. Once a year there would be a very large fayre on Black Heath Common. At the far end of the Common, I can remember a set of very large iron gates, leading to the road, and a row of houses either side. That's where an old boy would be selling hot chestnuts. He would be there every year. There was a tunnel or subway with a very large opening with white tiles and us kids would run to the other end, under the river Thames. We would come up where the barges are, at one end of Greenwich. We would spend all day mucking about by the river, and then walk home.

Alan lived in Brookdale Road, at the end of which was a large park encompassing the local dog stadium. In the evenings cars would draw up by the pavement, their occupants heading for the races. Alan would run up to the drivers, open the car door and say, 'Look after your car mister.' At the end of the evening they would come back to their vehicles and Alan would be standing guard. 'If they had a win,' he says, 'I would get about half a crown. No win, I would get a bob or nothing at all.'

Frank Hind recalls that most small boys had two or three Dinky toys, usually military vehicles, which they would tow along the pavement on a bit of string.

74 *The vestry of Morley Chapel School at Morley near Wilmslow had been closed for more than 25 years but was quickly made ready as a place where young children evacuated to the area could play.*

He also remembers playing marbles a lot, and particularly liked the ones made from coloured glass. These could be purchased in Taunton from a novelty shop, run by a 'little man with a broad Lancashire accent.' Frank later learnt that he was 'had up for selling pornography under the counter'! Frank also became proficient at making gliders out of stiff cardboard.

Despite the shortage of toys, there were many ways of acquiring secondhand ones. Relatives, neighbours and friends were always willing to pass on those their own children had grown out of, and children did not care in those days if they were brand new or not. One Christmas Anne Biffin's father managed to acquire a secondhand Hornby train set for her brother which the son of a colleague had outgrown. One of the rollers from a disused mangle ended up as the engine for a wooden train. Anne and her sister had a 'huge secondhand doll's house' themselves, which was acquired for them by an aunt. 'So, despite home made and secondhand toys we never felt deprived during those grim years.' Much of her very happy childhood, was spent walking in the countryside, picking wild flowers and swimming in the river Test.

Marilyn Wood grew up in Kettering. Her wartime childhood games fell into three categories, which she lists as seasonal, inherited and ephemeral. Seasonal games included whip and top, hoops and conkers; inherited ones involved the likes of skipping, jacks, hopscotch, and singing; whereas ephemeral games were often 'crazes' that sprang up from nowhere and disappeared within a few weeks. 'Although the first two types formed a constant background to my growing up,' she says, 'it was the third that can resurrect, even now, images and feelings from the past with greater accuracy. We did not know, nor particularly care, if similar sport existed in other parts of our town, or even throughout the country. When these ephemera appeared like mushrooms, overnight and secretly, we claimed them as our own and played them increasingly until, just as swiftly and secretly, they disappeared.'

One such game that sprang up in her neck of the woods in the early summer months of 1944 was cigarette, or 'fag', card flicking. At that time most children, both girls and boys, possessed a horde of cigarette cards, gleaned from adult smokers or family acquaintances. These colourful snippets of information covered a wide variety of subjects, including history, science, geography, biology and botany. For those who bothered to study the pictures and read the short paragraphs on the back, they became a source of general knowledge far beyond anything taught in the local primary school. As with all collections there were many cases of duplicated cards. In Marilyn's case it was 'Veronica Lake, whose one eye peered provocatively out at the world, the other being

75   *Learning can be fun. A typical 'Baby Walker' from the 1940s.*

76   *Most children had a collection of cigarette cards. These pages are from books accompanying two very popular series from the late 1930s. 'Wild Flowers' issued by W.D. & H.O. Wills, and 'RAF Badges' issued by John Player & Sons.*

permanently hidden by a cascade of hair.' She also remembers a superfluity of Captain Webb, Rolls-Royce and ox-eye daisies. Her main collection was stored in a biscuit tin in her bedroom, the 'swaps huddled together within the confines of an elastic band'. She explains that:

> The venue for this flicking competition was a small row of terraced houses at right angles to my own street, the appointed time after tea. About half past five I wandered along, my bundle of duplicates in my pocket. Four boys I recognised from a higher class at school had set out their individual pitches, on the pavement beneath the front windows of the houses, well removed from each other. A group of children was already gathered but this was definitely a one to one game. The rules were simple, each player had to stand on the kerb to flick, a card had to cover more than half the one on which it landed and it had to be picture side up to win. Most of the girls just threw a card more in hope than expectation of it landing correctly; the boys developed aerodynamic tricks by bending corners, or they tried to bounce the card off the wall onto the chosen prize. No one method appeared to outstrip the others when it came to winning. Like autumn leaves the multi-coloured cardboard rectangles fell to earth, the majority face downwards. Occasionally, there would be a shout of delight as a flick managed to meet all the requirements expected of a winner, then one or sometimes a small pile of cards would be eagerly scooped up. As dusk fell, however, only the four boys running the game returned home with a large increase in their stock.

Over the course of the summer Marilyn managed to send her duplicate Veronica Lakes and other cards to new homes and in return welcomed Tyrone Power, Roy Rogers, Ivor Novello, new inventions and exotic birds and animals into her biscuit tin. It was all-absorbing while it lasted. Then, suddenly, it was all over. Children still collected cigarette cards, still increased their store of general knowledge, but returned to exchanging 'swaps' in the more mundane, time-honoured manner.

Of course, during the war many boys collected anything to do with the military. Fathers and uncles might give them things, and the rest they would scrounge from troops stationed near their homes. In Dorset, Roy Stevens and his brother had a collection of army cap badges. Pride of place went to a large silver-coloured badge of the Argyll and Sutherland Highlanders. 'These badges were quite easy to come by,' he claims, 'as the south coast was one vast concentration area in the lead up to D-Day. We also had a small collection of shrapnel and some twisted pieces of aluminium from a downed German plane.'

In Devizes, Bill Underwood recalls that collecting shrapnel fragments from bombs or bits of downed aircraft was also popular at his school. The most highly prized pieces were taken from German aircraft, but these were very difficult to obtain, because crash sites were always guarded by armed sentries. Fragments of parachutes would occasionally surface in the classroom.

The war also induced an interest in adventures with military themes. The war games played by Donald Raine and his friends, for instance, involved building make-believe aircraft, tanks or warships in his father's garage, using any materials that came to hand. Inside these they would have 'up-to-date maps' of the regions involved in the war. One week they might be fighting a tank battle in Libya, or sailing in a warship on the Atlantic, and the next taking part in the bombing of Berlin. Donald kept up with the progress of the war by listening to the radio news or reading daily papers. When it snowed, some of the mothers made their sons white battledresses for the Russian front, so they could attack the big house at the end of the road, although all too soon these adventures were brought to an abrupt end by their mothers calling 'Dinner's ready'!

Colin Russell and his friends would imagine they were in the various armed forces. Gel, being older, usually played the part of a senior officer and marched the younger ones up and down the road. They would chalk stripes, pips or rings on to their clothes. After being promoted numerous times, the sleeves of jackets and jumpers would be covered with chalk, much to the annoyance of mothers.

Explorer and mountaineer Chris Bonington was already dreaming of adventures while at school, and describes how one game played by him and his friends got them into a spot of bother.

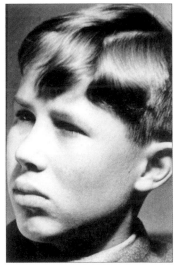

As a child I was a great escaper, no doubt showing signs of a future adventurous spirit. At the age of eight, I was at a little boarding school near Kirkby Lonsdale in Westmorland. It was in a big mock-Gothic mansion, which perhaps reminded us of Colditz, though the school itself was very pleasant indeed. It was, of course, during the war, and perhaps

77   Chris Bonington who spent the war at a boarding school in Westmorland.

this was what encouraged us to make a great escape. Half a dozen of us first hoarded food – bacon rinds, bacon fat from the dishes and then a fruit cake and malt loaf which the headmistress had prepared for a tea party for some parents visiting the school. We slipped away with our iron rations with no real idea of where we were going to go. I think we walked about three miles and then settled down to play by some trees and a culvert under the small country road. As twilight came, and we had finished our iron rations, the adventure was wearing a little thin. The prospect of spending the night in a tree, for fear of being attacked by wild animals, didn't seem at all attractive. We were just starting to walk back to school when the headmistress, who had been combing the countryside in her car, came across us. As a punishment, we had to stay behind when the rest of the school all went to the theatre in Kendal. We had a lovely evening, I remember, in the room of the school matron, who had had to stay behind to look after us, with her telling us stories by a roaring fire. This was the first of my adventures.

In 1939 Frank Hind's maternal grandmother gave him a fine new tricycle with pneumatic tyres, which he rode around their large garden endlessly. When he started school in 1942 he rode the tricycle to the edge of town and left it with an elderly couple who worked on his grandfather's farm. He would then catch the bus to the other side of town, a green single-decker with a gas fuel trailer behind. When Frank was eight he was given a secondhand bicycle which was slightly too big for him, so he had to have wooden blocks fitted to the pedals to start with. He cleaned it up, painted it, obtained some dynamo lights, and thereafter rode the three miles across town to school and back every day. This was the beginning of a lifelong love of cycling.

Doreen Govan also remembers the 'big day' when she got her first bike! Of course, most metal at this time was used in the manufacture of war equipment so very few new bikes were made. However, her father had put her name down on a list for any new bikes that became available. Her turn came so with great excitement Doreen and her father went 'Down Town to the bike shop to collect it' from what must have been one of the few shops in Bristol that had not been bombed. It was a girl's Raleigh bike, painted black because other colours were not permitted in wartime, but Doreen was thrilled to bits. Her school friend Sheila, who lived on the other side of Bristol, had a black Sunbeam, so endless possibilities opened up for the friends. 'Not only could we ride to school and back,' says Doreen, 'but there was the occasional treat of stopping for week-ends at each others houses.'

78   *Small comfort! The Chubb boys, three brothers evacuated from Acton to the village of Holbeton in Devon, clutching their teddy bears.*

The war years were a time of improvisation when it came to children's toys and games, and the same philosophy applied at Christmas. Audrey Purser recalls that her family never had a proper Christmas tree throughout this time. They would go on to the Downs and pick branches off a fir tree to take home. These were placed in a pot and decorated with lots of cotton wool, for snow, and anything else to add a bit of seasonal colour. They also made paper chains and dotted holly around the house. 'I was so excited with everything I found in my stocking,' she recalls, 'an orange and apple (if we were lucky), pencil, nuts, marbles, a piece of coal for fun, a comb and whatever else you could get in the war.' Audrey always wanted a doll, but 'I never got one!'

Being Entertained and Informed

The cinema, or 'pictures' as it was widely termed, was very popular with children. Geoff Grater remembers children flocking to see westerns with the likes of Roy Rogers, Gene Autrey and Hopalong Cassidy on a Saturday afternoon.

79   *Frank Hind on his new tricycle with pneumatic tyres in 1939.*

> We queued up in the rain outside the cinema in Tiverton and bought a miniature penny loaf from the bakery opposite all hot out of the oven. The most amazing and also frustrating experience was when the film was reaching its climax and the villain being pursued by Hopalong Cassidy took refuge in a barn up in the rafters. Kids would be looking to see where he was and got their cap guns out to shoot the villain on the screen before Hoppy got to him. There was bedlam and this spoilt the dialogue at the most exciting part of the film. But you could not help laughing at the same time. And then when the lights came up they all rushed to the fire escape to avoid having to remain while the National Anthem was being played.

In Stroud, Pat Robinson tells us that, although there was already a Gaumont cinema in the town, a new Ritz opened in late August 1939. It was very smart and could seat 1,250 people. It also boasted a Cadena Café above the cinema. As this could be accessed from outside as well as from inside, non-cinema patrons could also use it and it became very popular for morning coffee. The Ritz was built for and owned by Mr Waters. With the arrival of evacuees it became popular, and soon there were Saturday morning film clubs for the children as well as Sunday screenings. In time, the Cadena Café became a British Restaurant, one of a series of establishments backed by the government and run by the council aimed at providing simple but nourishing and inexpensive meals.

From their farm outside of Taunton, Frank Hind and his mother employed a rather unusual mode of transport when attending the pictures. She never learnt to drive so they went everywhere in the pony and trap. 'She always had a pony,' he recalls, 'and did a lot of horse dealing during the war. On one occasion we were driving past the Odeon cinema with a new horse in the shafts when it took fright and kicked the front of the trap to smithereens! Mum soon sold that one. On another occasion, driving past a council estate, we were pelted with stones by a gang of evacuee urchins from London shouting, "Get the dirty gypsies!" Mum was not amused. Most weeks we went to the Gaiety cinema to see a Roy Rogers film and left the pony and trap tied up in a back street near the railway station.'

Naming children after movie stars was very popular. Deanna Allan, born in Corby on 10 June 1941, third daughter of Jack and Agnes Dixon, was so named because Deanna Durbin was starring in the film *Three Smart Girls* at the local Odeon and 'it seemed apt for Mum to name me after the leading lady'.

Even in remote parts of Scotland the pictures kept children entertained. At Avoch, Donald Patience remembers going to a hall in Fortrose to watch films, his favourites being Laurel and Hardy, Old Mother Riley and, once again, cowboy films. 'We used to make guns out of pieces of wood and play cowboys and Indians,' he writes.

Jean Pearse describes an incident when her future husband Roy and his brother Tony were at the Saturday morning children's cinema club at Kingsbridge in Devon, for which they paid threepence. On this particular afternoon, two hundred children had gathered to watch Sabu starring in *The Thief of Baghdad*. At one point Sabu climbed to the top of an idol to steal a jewel from its head. While he held the jewel in his hand there was a terrifying bang and plaster fell from the

80   *Frank Hind and his brother in their mum's trap. This was their mode of transport when going to the pictures in Taunton.*

ceiling of the cinema on to the children below. Someone shouted 'A bomb has been dropped across the road. Get out of the cinema.' Roy and Tony raced up Church Street, where they found that all the windows had been blown out of the houses. Three people had been killed in a building across the road from the cinema. How lucky the children of Kingsbridge were that day, as had the bomb hit the cinema it might have wiped out an entire generation in one go.

In south London, Mike Thomas recalls that after a bomb hit a cinema in Newington Butts and blew its roof off, the local kids invaded the stricken building to fool around on the old stage, while other kids threw stones at them. 'We were never hurt,' he states in their defence. Gerald Webb remembers being taken to the pictures at Fareham by his mother to see a Carmen Miranda film. The actress was famous for her outrageous head-wear, and on this occasion wore a towering hat decorated with fruit. The boy's eyes widened as he exclaimed, 'Look at all that fruit Mum!' His remark caused the adults in the audience to burst out laughing.

People say that music forms the soundtrack to your childhood, and this is particularly true of those who grew up in the war years. British musical artists of the time included Gracie Fields, Joe Loss and of course Vera Lynn, while after the Americans invaded Britain in 1942, they brought music with them that has become almost synonymous with the time. It was the age of 'Swing,' and artists like Glen Miller, Benny Goodman and Tommy Dorsey feature heavily in memories, as well as crooners such as Frank Sinatra and Bing Crosby. Music was important for many reasons, particularly as it raises people's spirits.

The mother of Ron Green, who lived in Norfolk, always maintained that the war years were 'the best of her life'. She would play the piano in a pub called the *Kimberley Arms*, once or twice a week, about two miles from their home in Wymondham. The children, including Ron, would accompany her through the quiet country lanes singing the popular songs of the day as they went along. Her repertoire included 'You are my Sunshine', 'Don't Fence me in', and 'Alone', a lesser known song from the time that appeared in the Marx brothers' film *A Night at the Opera*. Ron remembers returning home from the pub later in the evening, guided by the light of an old oil lamp. When they counted the money she'd earned after a hat was passed around, there may have been five shillings or more. It was usually enough to buy a KitKat bar, some chips, and a *Beano* comic for the kids.

Bill Underwood also lists many of the songs that were popular with wartime children, among them memorable titles like 'Roll out the Barrel', 'Wish me Luck as you Wave me Goodbye', 'I'll be Seeing You', 'Kiss me Goodnight Sergeant Major', 'It's a Lovely day Tomorrow', 'Don't sit under the Apple tree', 'Moonlight becomes You', 'I Couldn't Sleep a Wink last Night', 'Bless 'em All', 'I've got Sixpence', 'When they Sound the Last All Clear', 'Deep in the Heart of Texas', 'White Cliffs of Dover', 'White Christmas', 'Roll me Over', 'We'll Gather Lilacs', and 'Lille Marlene', adding, 'Songs were either heard on the wireless,' or heard being sung in the pubs.' But there were many others as well, including 'This is the Army Mr Jones', 'When the Lights Go On', 'Shine on Harvest Moon', 'Won't you Come Home Bill Bailey' and 'Bye Bye Blackbird'. Children adapted lyrics of some popular songs for the situation. One example went as follows: 'Whistle while you work, Mussolini made a shirt, Hitler wore it, Chamberlain tore it, whistle while you work.' Another variation of the same lyric proclaimed: 'Whistle while you work, Hitler is a twerp, He's half barmy, so's his Army, whistle while you work.' Then there was 'Underneath the spreading chestnut tree, Mr Chamberlain said to me, why don't you join the ARP, 'neath the spreading chestnut tree.' And of course there was the slightly naughtier 'Hitler has only got one ball, Goering has two but very small, Himmler has something similar, and poor old Goebbels has no balls at all!'

In Stroud, Pat Robinson explains there was also a demand for live entertainment and Sunday evening concerts were arranged by ENSA at the Ritz, which brought many well known radio artists to the town. Local people were also encouraged to perform, in shows known as 'Stroud Wartime Discoveries', for which auditions were held. For performers under the age of 16 there was 'Youth Takes a Bow'. Pat recalls that in her class at the High School there was a girl called Terry Waters, the daughter of the owner of the Ritz, who had a delightful voice and everyone agreed it was a special treat to hear her sing.

A lot of entertainment also took place in the home. At Bramley, Bill Johnson's house, The Knot, was a place where soldiers could dance in the lounge to a wind up gramophone during the evenings. Anybody in uniform was welcome, British, American, even Home Guard, although he has to admit that the attraction might not have been the music but his twin sisters Betty and Clare, who in 1943 joined the WRNS. They were known in the village as the 'Terrible Twins'. The house was

81 *When Ron Green lived in Wymondham in Norfolk, his mother played the piano in a pub called the* Kimberley Arms. *The children would accompany her the two miles through the quiet country lanes, singing the popular songs of the day.*

also used by the band of the Pioneer Corps to practise in, as they were billeted nearby. The ladies of the village turned the village hall into a canteen, open every evening and known locally as the Silver Slipper, it was here and in other halls that the Pioneer Corps band would often perform. Many of these musicians remained friends of the family long after the war and the drummer married Bill's sister Betty.

The BBC produced a range of music and comedy wireless programmes to help people through the day. In Swindon, Margaret Harber's family would listen to programmes like ITMA and Worker's Playtime, while Children's Hour was popular with many others. For some people, particularly in remote areas, the BBC was their only link with the outside world. They sat beside the wireless every day, waiting for the news or the speeches of various leaders. During the dark days of 1940, when the threat of imminent invasion hung over everyone, Roy Stevens recalls how in Broadstone his family would gather around the Cossor wireless set, which was his father's pride and joy, to listen to Churchill's evening broadcasts to the nation. No matter how grave the news the family was inspired, and the great man made them believe that, come what may, Britain would eventually prevail. 'As a result,' he says, 'there was never a feeling of defeatism, but always a quiet confidence that somehow we would pull through. I listened avidly to the news bulletins on the radio, following

82   *A large group of children from Croydon being entertained at a party provided by the business people of the town. Among them are helpers from the British Red Cross Society.*

the course of the war. I became fascinated by faraway places with strange sounding names where battles were raging: Tobruk, Mersa Matruh, Benghazi, Tripoli, Kharkov, Stalingrad and The Pripet Marshes are some that come to mind.'

Deanna Allan was only a very small child but was aware of the tension and stress felt by the women of the country. One of her earliest memories is of a nightly ritual held by her mother. She would listen intently to the nine o'clock news and then the shipping news, which listed Royal Navy and Merchant Navy ships lost at sea. 'We were not put into our nightdresses until Mother knew that Dad's ship had survived yet another day,' writes Deanna. 'I suppose we were kept in a state of readiness to flee along the blacked-out streets to my grandparents should the news be dire. Then she would line us up military style and on the command "By the right, quick march" we mounted the stairs like little soldiers, getting into bed all the happier for our mother's lighter mood.'

Some people would also listen to the Nazi propaganda broadcasts made by William Joyce. They were not interested in fascism, but the bulletins often provided news unobtainable from the BBC. Myra Williams notes that on one occasion after a German raid during which a graveyard at Bryn Amman was bombed, Lord Haw Haw's broadcast included the hope that the German bombs did not disturb the dead in that little graveyard in Wales. Obviously, the Germans had informers all over Britain able to provide Berlin with current information.

One morning Roy Stevens recalls how his school gathered to listen to a very important announcement over the school loudspeakers. 'As we sat there,' he explains, 'the BBC announced that earlier that morning Allied troops under the command of General Eisenhower had landed on the northern coast of France and established beach-heads. Young as we were, we understood that something momentous had happened and that victory would only be a matter of time.'

Uniformed Youth Clubs

With most men and many women either in the armed forces, or helping one of the civil defence organisations, uniformed youth clubs were very well supported. In fact they were encouraged by the government which established the National Advisory Youth Council, who in co-operation with the Board of Education, issued a directive enjoining local councils to create more boys' clubs and youth centres, and to expand the cadet organisations. Such clubs included the Army Cadet Force, Sea Cadet Corps and the Air Defence Corps, which in 1941 became the Air Training Corps. In public schools there was the Junior Training Corps. All these organisations were naturally male-orientated, but the recruitment of females into the armed forces led to the creation of the Girls' Training Corps, Women's Junior Air Corps, and Girls' Nautical Training Corps. Other children were drawn to more traditional clubs such as the Cubs, Scouts, Boys' Brigade, Brownies, Girl Guides, Junior Red Cross and St John Ambulance, to name a few.

At the start of the war Bill Underwood was a member of the Cubs, and in 1940, along with his friends Bernie Bishop and Don Slade, he progressed to the Boy Scouts. During the early summer of 1940 a group of Scouts including these three friends started to camp out behind Devizes Scouts Hall every night and go to school during the day. On Tuesday 26 June all were sleeping soundly in their

83   *A number of children are among the audience at a show for the benefit of people spending long hours in the night shelters provided by underground railway stations, in this case Aldwych.*

84   *One of Britain's top wartime entertainers, Gracie Fields, receives a bouquet of flowers and warm applause after a performance.*

tents when around 1am the air-raid siren went: the first one in Devizes. They all woke up, and then turned over and went back to sleep again. It wasn't long before Colonel Steele, the district Scouts leader, and Mr Slade, Den's father, came and woke them up and made them run to a nearby trench where they stayed until the all clear sounded.

As part of the war effort, the Scouts would go around the town collecting waste paper. When it was Bill and Bernie's turn they arrived at the Scouts Hall, with books they had chosen from the school library to read when time permitted. At the back of the hall was a large mulberry tree laden with fruit. 'The temptation was too great,' states Bill, and instead of paper collecting they put their books down on the grass and climbed the tree to sample the tasty mulberries. 'We were so busy enjoying these that we didn't notice Colonel Steele arrive'. Without them noticing, the Colonel removed their library books and locked them in the Scouts Hall before ordering the boys down from the tree and home. But instead of obeying his command they hid in some bushes and waited for the man to depart. 'When it was all clear,' continues Bill, 'we went back to the scene of the crime and Bernie bunked me up to a small open window from which I was able to reach down to open a larger one.' He managed to clamber into the hall and retrieve the library books. At the next Scouts evening, Colonel Steele took the boys' aside and told them to go home and never return. Two weeks later he repented and, visiting their homes, invited them back. 'Bernie went back,' notes Bill, 'but I refused and joined the Boys' Brigade who instead of collecting waste paper were busy collecting stinging nettles and rose-hips.'

In north London, Gerald Lettice was a member of the Boys' Brigade and in 1943 took part in the celebrations to mark the 60th anniversary of the founding of the organisation. This took place on the lawns inside Windsor Castle and included an inspection by King George VI. Gerald was a corporal in the Enfield Company and one of two representatives from his locality. The King, who Gerald says actually spoke to him, was dressed in the uniform of an army general and the two princesses were in bright pink.

At Wigston, Duncan Lucas was a member of his local Scouts group and recalls one Bank Holiday when preparing to go 'on a trek'. They were ready with their rucsacks and billy-cans, when an aeroplane flew overhead which one of the lads proclaimed to be a 'Hampden', a British bomber. But some amongst them had noted it had a tail-gun to the rear.

> Now a lad in the war years had to have a good knowledge of military aircraft. We lads were efficient at plane spotting and when we noticed the crosses on the wings shouted, 'It's a Jerry'. He did a bit of a dip and started to turn and we heard the 'crump crump' of the bombs. The plane turned and came back over us, we lads were yelling and swearing as it was the only weapons we had, then the sirens went and much to our disgust we were all rushed to a shelter at the side of Two Steeples factory where Chitham's offices now stand and for a considerable time we were kept in this shelter.

After the all clear, the Scouts were allowed out of the shelter but told to go home, the 'trek' having been cancelled because of the danger posed by the Germans. But instead they headed for Cavendish Road where they understood the bombs

85   *Army Cadet Force PT course at Winterbourne Gunner near Salisbury in June 1944. Bill Underwood is sitting at the far right.*

had been dropped. 'We were not allowed in the road,' he writes, as there was a soldier blocking their way with a rifle. So they approached by an alternative route along the alley of a pub. 'We came back into Cavendish Road,' he continues, 'and destruction was everywhere. I remember a whole row of houses with their roofs in the road, and an old woman dusting oranges, covered with glass and dust. It must have been early in the war years for oranges to be about.'

Sometime before the end of the war Mr Lucas found himself working as a bicycle messenger for the local Home Guard unit stationed at Aylestone Lane near the railway bridge. He explains that they slept in the 'old billiard hut at Uncle Les's yard.' On one occasion, during Home Guard manoeuvres, several Boy Scouts were given training with carrier pigeons. 'We were shown how to write the message and place it in a little capsule which was then attached to the pigeon's leg,' he describes. On the day of the manoeuvres it rained, so the Scouts wore their brilliant yellow capes to help protect them against the elements. Of course, they could be seen for miles so were ordered to remove them by the Home Guard officer, Mr Payne. Mr Lucas enlarges on what happened next:

> Suddenly, advancing up the fields were several lines of men. Soldiers with rifles held in front of them. They came up the fields at a steady march and made quite an imposing sight. At the footbridge 'Rally Bridge' to those who knew it well another group became active. We were told to go and find out what was happening so we could send our message. Instead of the words 'Enemy advancing in large numbers' we felt we should state the exact number of the enemy, but were soon told to obey orders and use the 'official jargon'. We sent the pigeon off, forgetting in our excitement to check for overhead wires fortunately, though the pigeon missed the wires. We then went down to the bridge to see what was happening. Throwing discretion to the winds, we walked across and saw a large machine gun being mounted on a tripod. Fire-crackers started to go off, all hell broke loose. One of the local Home Guards, who had got some blanks and had been itching to fire these off all day, slipped the first one 'up the spout' of his rifle and banged away happily. Men appeared all around. A soldier wearing a white armband with umpire on it and an agitated expression was shouting, 'You bloody fools, you're shooting at your own side'. Thank goodness it was only a practice!

In 1942 Bill Underwood left the Boys' Brigade to join the Army Cadet Force, of which he remained a member for the next two years. The CO was a Major Waylean, an ex Wiltshire Regiment officer. His only son, who was a major in the same regiment, was killed in the Sicily Landing. The cadets took part in one camp at Le Marchant Barracks and a PT course at Winterbourne Gunner on Salisbury Plain, where they spent their time doing assault courses and long marches. 'It put me in good stead when I did my National Service,' Bill admits. One day they marched from the Drill Hall in Devizes to Roundway Hill where the Americans gave them a demonstration of camouflage. They were also given rides in their tanks, which they found both exciting and frightening, tearing over the downs and going in and out of the chalk pits. Towards the end of the war he left the Army Cadets and joined the Air Training Corps for a while.

86   *Leeds Army Cadet Force 1945. The boy under the door knocker was Molly Kinghorn's suspected Canadian soldier.*

In Leeds, Molly Kinghorn was not in the cadets herself, but her friendship with a certain boy in the Army Cadets got local tongues wagging. One day she was confronted by her mother because a nosy neighbour had informed her that her daughter had been seen walking out with a Canadian soldier. Molly was only 12 at the time but admits to looking quite grown up. However, there was no truth in the story, which left both her and her mother puzzled. 'It was some weeks later,' she recalls, 'that I remembered walking home from school one day with a boy in the cadets whose uniform had Army Cadet Force on the sleeve.' The word 'Cadet' had no doubt been mistaken for 'Canada' by the nosy neighbour.

At Avoch, Donald Patience joined the Air Training Corps when he was old enough and spent hours poring over the silhouettes of German and Allied planes. He also learned navigation and sat exams. In Bristol, Doreen Govan went to the Girl Guides every Tuesday and a youth club run by the chapel every Friday. 'We also had a thriving Boys' Brigade,' she claims, 'so the social whirl for teenagers began to take shape.'

Although from Tottenham, Peter Richards was evacuated privately to Northampton, to attend Kilburn Grammar School, which was then using the premises of Northampton Town and County School in the afternoons. He was 12 at the time and decided to join the local Boys' Brigade, where he learnt First Aid to the Injured. This was to become very important in his future life. In February 1941

87   *June Van Dam and her sister belonged to the Brownie pack at Hutton in Essex.*

88 *Barbara Raine, with bouquet and floral patterned dress, Brownie Queen 1945, outside Wibsey Methodist church.*

he returned to Tottenham, and started at Tottenham Grammar School. As well as keeping up his membership of the Boys' Brigade, he joined the St John Ambulance Brigade as an ambulance cadet, later achieving the rank of corporal. He eventually joined the senior brigade as an ambulance man, and regularly spent nights at the North Middlesex Hospital performing all sorts of duties, mainly as a messenger boy.

> I remember a number of elderly patients arriving from a bombed out hospital in west London, and we had to transfer them to the wards. In so doing I successfully jammed a lift; thus we had to carry these people, mainly ladies in chairs, and manhandle them up the steps. My name was rather murky among some friends in the British Red Cross who were there at the time and attended the same church as I did.

Hazel Reigate lived in Sanderstead and was a member of the Croydon junior detachment of the British Red Cross Society. On first joining there was no red cross on your apron, and in order to earn it, she had to take a series of exams

89 *The junior detachment of the British Red Cross Society marching through Croydon around 1940. Hazel Reigate, pictured on the end of the fourth row, admits to being the only girl out of step. Note that the girls have not yet earned their red crosses.*

90   *Hazel Reigate wearing her British Red Cross Society peaked cap, in November 1940. She still has the cap today.*

in First Aid, Home Nursing, Child and Infant Welfare, and Resuscitation of the apparently drowned. She was very busy most evenings helping out in local hospitals or at the old persons home, assisting a lady with seven children, or working in the Red Cross headquarters packing parcels for troops overseas. She might also be on duty at public events, just in case anybody needed first aid.

Not all children joined uniformed organisations, and there were many other clubs and societies to entertain them. For instance in Kent, Allan George

91   *Hazel Reigate (second from left) has now won her red cross. During a field day to raise money for the British Red Cross Society, Hazel won a prize for being the only perfectly dressed girl. 'Notice collar position,' she explains.*

recalls that the Faversham Youth Centre had been opened during the war and, among other activities, had a very lively drama group. The local ARP warden suggested they should attempt their first pantomime, explaining that very few of the local children, had ever had the opportunity to enjoy such a show. So, with the help of the headmistress from the primary school as producer, the club staged 'Cinderella' in the Faversham Boys Grammar School gymnasium during February 1945. The event would continue for many years. It must have been a wonderful diversion for the children, bringing them happiness and hope in austere times.

Chapter 7

Escaping the Bombs

It was generally feared that Germany's attack on Britain would include the indiscriminate bombing of civilian targets, as had already been witnessed during the Civil War in Spain, where in April 1937 the Condor Legion attacked the Basque town of Guernica on a busy market day. Some time prior to hostilities the British government drew up plans to evacuate school children from hazardous zones. The idea was to move evacuees from the cities to areas of safe haven in the countryside. Much of the work would be organised and undertaken by local authorities and the Women's Voluntary Service. The first evacuation commenced on 1 September 1939, and within four days more than 1,300,000 individuals had been moved out of London alone. Children left their homes and headed into the unknown, carrying little more than their gas mask and a suitcase.

The Evacuation Scheme

Although now a suburb of Leicester, Wigston was decidedly more rural at the time, and a typical reception area for London evacuees. The Government Evacuation Scheme was first drawn up in 1937, and J. R. Colver of the Greater Wigston Historical Society has studied it:

> Described by the then Minister of Health, Mr Walter Elliott, as potentially an exodus bigger than the one of Moses, the voluntary evacuation from the cities and towns of one and a half million women and children was first discussed by the Committee of Imperial Defence in 1937. It had been assumed that an air attack on London would be a continuous affair from the onset of war and that more than half a million people would be killed with double that number injured in the first two months.

In order to prepare the people of Wigston for this influx a practice was held on 1 August 1939. Eight hundred children from five local schools assembled at 3.20pm on the platform at Wigston Magna train station, where the Chief Reception Officer and his two assistants were distinguishable by white armlets containing the words 'Reception Officer'. Their first job was to either telephone or send messengers to the reception depots at Long Street School in Wigston Magna and South Wigston Modern School, five minutes after the train carrying the children had arrived. Also present at the station were three or four uniformed police constables and a qualified nurse with an assistant ready to attend to any medical emergencies. Buses belonging to the Midland Red Bus Company would be waiting at the reception depots to ferry children to their final destinations. The children themselves would

92   *Rehearsal for evacuees arriving at Wigston Magna train station on 1 August 1939.*

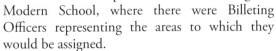

be accompanied by their own teachers, who would help to maintain good order throughout this transfer.

When all the children were assembled on the platform and ready to move off, the Chief Reception Officer gave a blast on a whistle which was the signal for them to head off in procession to the reception depots. The first 150 children marched in an orderly fashion to Long Street School and would be billeted in the area of Wigston Magna Urban District Council; they were met by the Chief Billeting Officer attached to them. The remainder proceeded to South Wigston Modern School, where there were Billeting Officers representing the areas to which they would be assigned.

At the reception depots, three-quarters of an hour was allowed for the consumption of a light meal and a brief medical inspection. After that buses would ferry the children to their respective destinations, although it is not quite clear how they were allocated accommodation. In some of the accounts we have, who went where seems to have been settled on an *ad hoc* basis.

In Bradford, seven-year-old Donald Raine took part in a similar exercise. He and his brother Gerald were among a throng of children who

93   *Two little Londoners at a railway station with gas mask and suitcase, about to depart for their reception area.*

walked from Bradford Grammar School to Forster Square railway station. This was in preparation for the day when they would be sent as evacuees to Giggleswick Grammar School near Settle. However, when it was time for the real thing Donald's mother decided that he was too young to leave home, although the older Gerald did indeed spend several months at Giggleswick before returning home as the bombers failed to materialise.

Following these rehearsals, the arrival of real evacuees was dealt with smoothly and efficiently. At Wigston, the first batch of genuine evacuees left London on 1 September 1939, and an entry made by the Clerk to the Council on that day notes that 'One train arrived. Approx 700 school children. None retained at Wigston, except one boy ill.' An entry on 2 September reads, 'One train arrived. Approx 650 mothers and children. About 100 retained at Wigston.' And on 3 September a further entry notes, 'One train arrived. Approx 650 mothers and children. 4 cases ill. All retained at Wigston.' Presumably there were no major incidents, as these would surely have been duly recorded. J. R. Colver explains that a great many rural areas were ill equipped to deal with this influx of people and writes, 'A shortage of suitable housing, schools and medical facilities were advanced but fell on the deaf ears of a government who had no alternative but to put their plans into operation.'

Officially, there were four groups of people evacuated: school children, accompanied only by their teachers; mothers with young children; expectant mothers and others with medical problems; and the blind, crippled and mentally ill. But there were problems. Colver notes that some people looked on evacuation as the chance of a free holiday, whilst others who had originally declined to take part clambered aboard buses that contained friends and neighbours because they suddenly felt they were missing out on an opportunity. 'Often potential foster parents,' continues Mr Colver, 'called at the reception centres to take possession of those children with the most appeal, not unnaturally the cleanest, best dressed and best spoken, leaving the billeting officers facing a problem with the unwanted, not easily dealt with, individuals.' There was a billeting allowance per child of eight shillings and sixpence a week or ten shillings and sixpence for those over 16 years. For a mother and child a lodging allowance of eight shillings was the modest compensation. Later, parents were made to pay six shillings towards the upkeep of each child.

How was everyone informed of the evacuation scheme? Arrangements were different around the country, but in Rosyth near Edinburgh Vena Bartlett recalls that the schools were issued with leaflets which were sent to all parents, advising them that evacuation of children to country areas would be the best means of keeping them safe. Because of its naval connections Rosyth was an obvious target for the enemy. She writes:

> Naturally this fell as an advance bombshell upon the thousands of homes in the city and caused much heartbreak and worry for all concerned. My parents were no exception and my mother was distraught at the prospect of 'that delicate little Vena' and her son being wrenched away from her. However, Dad persuaded her that it would be the correct thing to do, despite the agony of parting with the children, and might possibly save their lives. This argument couldn't be countered and the die was cast.

94   *First day of war. On the evening of 3 September 1939, a German submarine sank the liner* Athenia, *on its way from Liverpool to Montreal. Many of the 112 people who died were either refugees or American students returning home. In this picture a boy arrives in Galway with other weeping survivors aboard a Norwegian tanker.*

95   *Seventy-seven British children were drowned when the* City of Benares *evacuation ship was sunk by the Germans on 23 September 1940 on its way to Canada, thereby bringing the overseas evacuation scheme to an end. Five of the survivors, still managing to smile, are safe aboard a rescue ship.*

There were three principal periods of evacuation. The first began just before the declaration. The second was at the start of the London Blitz in September 1940 and occurred because most of the original evacuees had returned home after little bombing of civilian targets took place. The third major outflow happened in the advent of the flying bomb attacks in June 1944, because once again many people had drifted back after the end of the heavy raids in May 1941.

As war took hold in Europe, many continental children took refuge in Britain. They arrived from countries such as France, Belgium, Poland and Holland. Many had fled from Franco's Fascist regime in Spain. Then there were Jewish children sent to escape persecution at the hands of the Nazis. Over a million Jewish children would be murdered during the Holocaust. But, also, many British children were themselves sent overseas as a number of friendly foreign governments, including the United States and Canada, agreed to take large numbers. This was a very dangerous undertaking, as some of the ships that carried them across the Atlantic were attacked by German E-Boats, and after 77 British children were drowned when the *City of Benares* was sunk, the overseas evacuation scheme was discontinued.

Leaving London Behind

Norman Pirie and his younger broth-er were among the first evacuees who left London on 1 September 1939. They lived in a district called Euston House, about half a mile north of the Royal Victoria Dock. Norman was looking forward to starting grammar school, but because his brother had been unwell his mother insisted he accompany the school he had just left, in order to keep an eye on him. The school was sent by train to Portland in Dorset, but the choice of location was not a wise one. Portland was the home of a major naval base as well as being close to the Whitehead Torpedo factory

96   *After the initial phase, 200 London schools remained open for more children and parents to register for evacuation.*

at Weymouth, and when France fell and German aircraft were poised only sixty miles away, it was heavily bombed. After one particular raid on 4 July 1940, during which Jack Mantle won a posthumous VC aboard HMS *Foylebank*, Norman's parents took the brothers home again as London had not yet been attacked.

Also among this first wave of children to be evacuated from London was the entertainer Bruce Forsyth, who wrote of his experiences:

> When war was declared in 1939 I was eleven years of age and I had just started High School (The Higher Latymer in Edmonton). Almost immediately we were all evacuated to Clacton-on-Sea, leaving our parents in London. Unfortunately, I was billeted on my own with an old lady. She was very sweet but I was so homesick and felt terribly alone. At the weekend, my mother and father came to see if I was alright. When they arrived, I ran to the car, got in and wouldn't

get out. I cried and cried and cried. My father drove the car to the seafront and when they saw a warship just off Clacton Pier, they thought I was nearer the war than they were. They decided to take me home, to my delight, as I could watch all the air raids and aerial dog fights in the sky.

Winifred Taylor also lived near the Royal Docks in the Custom House area. One day in September 1939 she was told to report to her school with some clothes in a bag and her gas mask. When she arrived, all the other children were sitting in the playground having labels tied through their buttonholes with their names on them. Their relatives were congregating in the street outside the school, but she did not know why. Eventually, all the children with their families following were marched to Plaistow Station. 'I remember a lot of crying,' she recalls, 'as our families were not allowed on the platform.' The children were each given little bags of food to eat and then taken by train to Paddington Station, before setting off on another train to Bath in Somerset, where they were ushered into a schoolroom. Here they

were given another bag of food before boarding coaches that would ferry them to temporary homes, or 'billets' as they became known. Mrs Taylor admits the people she was billeted with were very kind, but she was so distressed they were unable to console her, and it was decided to return her home after only two weeks, although her brother remained.

Winifred would be evacuated again later in the war, to Radstock in Somerset during the Blitz, but this time the experience was very different. They were first taken to the school, where local people picked those they wanted, the rest, including herself, remaining

97   *A nurse at a welfare centre in one of the reception areas enters the details of a child evacuated from London.*

behind. She then recalls a procession of children being marched up and down the Somerset hills, as teachers went from house to house asking if anyone was prepared to accept a child. She was among the last to be accommodated. An elderly woman agreed to take a small girl, who was about six years old, so the teacher asked her if she would take Winifred too, to help her look after the girl. 'She did,' Winifred explains, 'but this was the start of a bad memory. The old lady's daughter who lived close by took a dislike to me and made my life hell. I was there for six months before I ran away. I was picked up in the early hours of the morning in an air-raid shelter in Bath, and when my mother was told, she took me home.'

Another person who found herself caught up in the evacuation of London was actress Dame Eileen Atkins, who writes:

> When I was five I'd been at school for I think about one week when the Second World War started. I was evacuated along with thousands of other school children. Our school was sent to Great Baddow in Essex and we all

stood there in a cluster, our gas masks hanging across us, clutching a bar of chocolate we'd all been given. We were paraded round the village and people came to their gates and chose a child. I was the first to be chosen but the woman didn't want my brother. He, with his best friend, was the last to be chosen. The woman who took them in said, when she saw them 'Oh dear, I said girls. I only wanted girls'. My brother said, 'Please take us lady, we're ever so clean'. He had found a home with the best family in Great Baddow – they had four girls and, now in his seventies, he's still friendly with them. As soon as I got through the door of my home from home, the woman's own daughter snatched my chocolate and punched and kicked me. So I screamed. I screamed until they said they'd get my mother. My mother came down and got me re-housed. She went home. I cried. I was sent to school and was found to have nits. I cried. They finally sent for my mother again. She took me home. I was sent to school in Tottenham. It was a very rough school. I cried. So my mother kept me at home. It wasn't discovered until I was nearly eight that I wasn't going to school.

Ted Hedges was ten years old at the time of the V2 rockets in 1944 and he was sent from Paddington Station with no idea of where he was going. All he carried was a pillowcase containing a few meagre belongings. The children arrived in the village of Tumble in South Wales during the evening and were taken, as far as he recalls, to a local school or village hall. Here local people were choosing which child they wanted. The hall gradually emptied of children, until Ted was the only one left. However, he explains, 'the cavalry' arrived in the form of an old gentleman called Willie John, who he observed speaking with those in authority. He did not speak to the boy, but simply took hold of his hand and led him out of the room. Ted soon realised that Willie did not speak English or, more likely, would not speak English. 'I had arrived in Wales,' states Ted, 'or more precisely Upper Tumble.'

He trusted the man who was taking him who knew where? It was dark when they arrived at a bungalow, which he was ushered inside to be met by a most welcoming lady, whom he would have loved to have been the grandmother he never knew. She took his pillowcase and that was the last he saw of it until he was eventually sent home to London.

There was a farm nearby and the farmer's son Raymond was given the task of befriending the young swallow. His first job was to get Ted out of the way long enough for Mrs Jones, the lady who lived in the house, to go through his few belongings. 'Take him up to the Craig', she told Raymond, which was an extensive jumble of boulders that in time Ted would cross every Saturday to collect eggs for the family. When he returned to the bungalow a bath was waiting and it was at that instant Ted felt 'safe and happy'. He was next put into the largest bed he had ever seen. It belonged to Aaron, the son of Mr and Mrs Jones, who was aged about 20 and worked as a miner. They would thereafter share the bed, but neither party seemed to mind the arrangement. Mr Jones himself was a police constable, and Ted admits that he came to 'love and respect' him. 'I have read and heard horrendous stories of evacuees being abused, underfed, and generally neglected,' states Ted. 'Not in my case: it was the most satisfying experience of my young

98   *Children from a school in East Ham evacuated to Bacton in Suffolk enjoying the heavy snow falls of the winter of 1939-40.*

life.' He particularly remembers the uncomfortable and weird sensation of wearing clogs and seeing Mrs Jones's pleasure the first time he mumbled some Welsh words – 'something about Willie John wanting to see her'.

When the time came for Ted to return to London in June 1945, Mr and Mrs Jones had got so attached to him they did not want him to leave. 'Mr Jones said a strange thing to me,' Ted recalls, suggesting that if he stayed in Tumble he could take cornet lessons. 'Perhaps he thought that would tip the balance.' But inevitably he had to return to his family in London and did so healthy and well nourished and, in his words, 'not the urchin' he started out as.

Jack Davie was also evacuated to Wales when he was nine years old. He remembers climbing aboard a great steam train at Paddington Station without any notion of where he was heading. The train journey lasted nearly all day and the first shock came at Llanelli where he was separated from his sisters who were taken out of the carriage and off the train. He, along with some other children, was then taken to a small village called Pumpsaint, where they climbed on to a bus to be delivered to the families that had agreed to foster them. Jack was to stay with the Lloyds and their house had no electricity or water. Oil lamps were used for lighting and water was collected from a well. The toilet was a bucket in a little shed in the garden, where cut up newspapers nailed to the door was used instead of toilet tissue. It was a predominantly Welsh-speaking area surrounded by mountains, so everything felt very strange to the young boy, but everyone was very friendly and they were gradually able to understand each other and talk together.

On the morning after they arrived the children were rounded up and shown the way to school. It was in the next village and attendance required a two-mile trek. The school provided a separate classroom for the London children and their own English teacher. Jack enjoyed the daily walk and soon made some good friends with whom he would go fishing and catch rabbits. Mr Lloyd would sometimes take him for rides on his motorbike and managed to find out where his sisters were staying, so took him to visit them on several occasions. Jack stayed with the Lloyds for about two years but when it was time for him to move up to senior school he was relocated to a family at Narbeth in Pembrokeshire. The school was called Greenwich Central and everybody spoke English. There were makeshift classrooms in various parts of the town, and a long walk between each lesson. Local farmers would ask for boys to go potato picking, which Jack agreed to do as he saw this as a chance to skive off a few lessons. At fifteen he eventually went back to London and was horrified by the devastation.

Philip Everest was evacuated to Crowborough in Sussex from his London home when he was six years old and it was not a particularly pleasant experience. Every morning he was fed in the scullery on porridge made in a big iron saucepan, and if for any reason the lady of the house was displeased with him he 'lost' a spoonful. He did not stay at this house for long, and was moved to another cottage in Crowborough on the edge of Ashdown Forest, with a single mother who had a 17-year-old daughter and a 12-year-old son. It was here that his troubles really began. The daughter had a sadistic streak and her bullying of him included burning his skin with a cigarette. One incident that disturbed him greatly was being forced to climb a tree to fetch a baby magpie from out of its nest. The girl proceeded to cut its tongue, believing for some bizarre reason that this would make it talk, as magpies are reputed to be able to mimic.

Living near an American army camp, the young mother would go out to the local pub on Saturday nights leaving her daughter in charge of their evacuee. One night the pair heard an 'unearthly scream' from outside. The girl sprang up and seized a poker, and arming Philip with another rushed outside and along the path, where they discovered the mother 'sprawled out on the grass with her clothes in disarray.' In the distance a soldier was seen making his escape. The following morning they were asked to attend an identity parade at the camp, but Philip cannot remember the outcome of this, or exactly what took place, although he is quite certain that if the girl had caught the American at the time, she would have killed him with the poker then and there.

99 *Doreen Shephard, front row third from left, with other evacuees from East Ham, in the playing field of their new school in Bacton, Suffolk.*

Even at eight or nine, he was aware that the daughter often acted in a provocative manner while they waited up for the mother to come home. It was nothing physical, he explains, but there were a lot of sexual connotations to the language she used. He was terrified of being alone with the girl and believes the experiences did him a great deal of harm.

Philip was later moved to what he terms a 'posh hole' in South Wales, where for the first time in his life he had his very own room. He was happy for a while, but began to have nightmares. As these got progressively worse it was decided to move him to be with his sister in another house in the same town. 'There was no cruelty here,' he confirms, 'but the house seemed to be full of people and kids, so you had to fend for yourself.' In time Philip and his sister returned home to London and he believes the experiences he had during evacuation affected his subsequent adult life, in which he suffered 'many bad years'. Now in his seventies, with six married sons and lots of grandchildren, he says, 'I have found peace of mind. I look back and see that every experience was a lesson for which I am thankful.'

Another London evacuee, Mike Thomas, also experienced abuse at the hands of a foster mother. In 1944 he found himself in a village called Marsh Gibbon in Buckinghamshire, where he was billeted with the stationmaster and his wife. Being 12 years old, he really enjoyed being around trains and was often allowed to travel on the footplate back and forth from Poundon Station. After a while the stationmaster's wife started to ill-treat him, throwing him up against the walls of the house and hitting him around the head. Mike complained to the stationmaster, but his wife always denied it. It was a traumatic time anyway, as his mother was in a sanatorium suffering with TB, from which she subsequently died.

The six-year-old brother of Peter Cattermole was a very boisterous child. His behaviour caused disruption when he was evacuated in 1942, along with his

100 *Children from Hungerford Road School in north London, who were evacuated to Wembdon in Somerset. Classes were held in the old vicarage and the teacher in this photograph taken in 1941, was Mr Norman.*

101   *This photograph was taken in the grounds of the old Vicarage in Wembdon, Somerset, in August 1940, and shows evacuated pupils of Hungerford Road School, north London. School master Mr Ford is at left, Mr Norman at right, and the headmaster Mr Hurley in centre.*

older brother and a large number of other children, from Ealing to Mirfield in Yorkshire. After being selected by a couple in a large public hall, the two brothers accompanied them to their house together. But after a few weeks, thanks to his younger brother's behaviour, they were separated. The brother went to a home in Skipton and Peter was sent to a place called Hackenthorpe Hall near Beighton Colliery. 'This residence had many boys of a similar age,' he explains, 'but what surprised us most was that it was run by firemen, which remains a mystery to this day.' Peter admits to enjoying his time at Hackenthorpe Hall. 'The staff kept us well organised,' he continues, 'with sports activities and outings, and we attended a lovely village school which made us very welcome.' Despite all this, life at the Hall in the charge of firefighters was not to every child's liking, and it was not uncommon for homesick boys to run away and try to return to London. 'Most were caught and brought back,' he points out. Even though it was a considerable distance, Peter's parents managed to visit him on a couple of occasions, and in 1944, although it still was not safe in Ealing, his father decided to take his sons home, where they remained until the end of the war.

Of National Concern

Not only London was affected by the evacuation scheme, other cities and large industrial towns being perceived as among Germany's targets. On Friday 1 September 1939, Alan Cairns and his elder brother boarded a train at Southampton bound for Andover along with other evacuees. Alan was nine years old and attending Highfield Church of England School, while his older brother was at Itchen Secondary School. Highfield was evacuated to a village called Appleshaw in Hampshire, but Alan's parents chose to send him with the secondary school pupils so he could be with his brother. They did not stay with their foster parents long, as the feared bombing of Southampton was slow in coming, and on Alan's tenth birthday, 21 December 1939, they returned home. Highfield School re-opened in January 1940 for part-time education, so Alan attended a few hours each day. Then the bombing began and he spent many nights in the Anderson shelter in the garden. The most memorable nights of the Southampton Blitz, he says, were

Saturday 23 November, Saturday 30 November, and Sunday 1 December, when much of the city was destroyed.

In the summer of 1941 he sat and passed the scholarship, which was subsequently replaced by the 11-plus in 1944. This enabled him to attend his local grammar school, Taunton's School, founded in 1760 by Southampton wine merchant Alderman Richard Taunton. Since September 1939, Taunton's School had been evacuated to Bournemouth to share the premises of the existing Bournemouth School, so for Alan this necessitated a second period of evacuation. He did not start there until 1941, but he explains what happened during the original evacuation.

> Of the 760 boys registered at the Taunton's School building in Highfield, now used by Southampton University, more than 600 were evacuated to Bournemouth, whose citizens were cooperative in providing billets for their young guests while acting as foster parents. The young Tauntonians were transported in two large groups from Southampton Central Station on Saturday 2 September 1939 on trains departing at 10.30am and 12.30pm. At Bournemouth School the first major task for the two headmasters, Mr J.E. Parry from Bournemouth and Mr F.J. Hemmings of Taunton's, was to inaugurate a workable education system for more than 1,200 of the host pupils and their wartime guests. For the first two terms, leading up to Christmas 1939 and then on to the spring of 1940, one school occupied the building each morning for a week with the other school using it in the afternoons. Saturdays were included and this routine was recognised as 'two-thirds education' and with extra homework enforced.

102   *Two girls evacuated from a school in Salford, Greater Manchester, arrive at their new home in Blackpool.*

In May 1940 a new system was introduced. One week the Bournemouth boys would have the classrooms in the mornings for academic subjects such as English, History, Geography and Mathematics, while the Taunton's pupils would use the laboratories and workshops for practical classes such as Chemistry, Physics, Art and Woodwork. In the afternoons, the procedure would be reversed. The following week the Bournemouth pupils would have the practical rooms in the mornings and the Taunton's boys the classrooms. This system was accepted as being the most beneficial for both schools and remained in place until the end of the evacuation period in March 1945. The only interruption to the routine came in early June 1940 when, for a few weeks after Dunkirk, approximately 800 French soldiers were billeted in the school buildings, followed by around 400 British troops.

103   *Pupils marching into chapel at Bisley School.*

Gerald Poole was evacuated to Bisley School in Surrey, home to children up to the age of 14, after which they transferred to Shaftesbury House, about three miles away. Both schools came under the combined heading of Arethusa Training Ship, children sometimes being sent here from homes with divorced parents. Gerald's own mother had four youngsters and a job testing double-decker buses at Leatherhead Bus Garage, so she found it difficult to cope.

At Bisley there were two dormitories, Trojans and Spartans. Gerald was a Trojan, and as such could learn one of several trades: shoemaking, tailoring, woodwork or engineering. He chose shoemaking, which became his profession when he left school in 1948. All the clothes and shoes the children wore were actually made at the school. At 14 he progressed to long trousers and Shaftesbury House, where the four dormitories were Cavaliers, Ironsides, Knights and Crusaders. Gerald was a Cavalier.

Life at Bisley was far removed from the war. There was a large playing field, where boys played football, cricket and athletics. There were also indoor games, such as badminton, snooker and billiards. The school band had about forty

104   *The Bisley School Band, which Gerald Poole remembers marching behind when attending chapel every Sunday morning and evening.*

105   *Pupils in the shoemaker's shop at Bisley School, where Gerald Poole learnt his adult trade.*

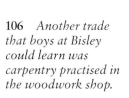

106   *Another trade that boys at Bisley could learn was carpentry practised in the woodwork shop.*

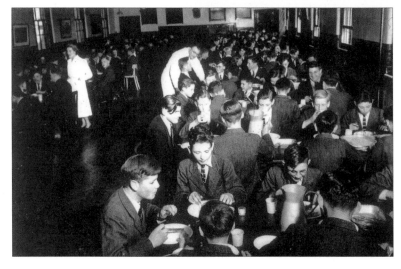

107   *In the dining hall at Bisley School.*

members, and Gerald remembers having to march behind it when he went to chapel every Sunday morning and evening. Highlights of the week were film nights on Wednesday and tuck shop opening hours on Saturdays. If you were naughty during the week an unpopular punishment was to miss the Wednesday film show. On Saturday morning everyone was given a dose of salts by Matron, after which there was a queue for the toilet.

Boys who were keen on gardening, as Gerald was, were given plots of land to grow vegetables, all of which were eaten at school. The dining hall could accommodate 200 lads and Gerald recalls that on the walls were roll of honour boards naming those who excelled in cricket and football. Gerald himself was in the physical training squad and during his time at the school went to the Royal Albert Hall on more than one occasion to do a display in front of the Queen and Princess Elizabeth. At Bisley one would hardly have known there was a war on if it hadn't been for the fact that Shaftesbury House was about two miles from the world famous Bisley Rifle Ranges and the children were often disturbed by the sound of rifle fire.

Doreen Foreman dates her evacuation to the time of Dunkirk. She was driven from her primary school to the railway station at Margate, which at the time was crowded with dishevelled soldiers, some on stretchers and others heavily bandaged. Ladies of the Red Cross were supplying the men with things like tea and sandwiches. Most of the men were Belgian or French, and one of them gave her a bar of chocolate. The children were taken to an unknown destination which turned out to be Rugeley in Staffordshire. They were lined up in a school playground for the foster parents to choose which they fancied. Doreen went to a miner's house, 'a complete contrast from home,' she points out. 'We were church goers; they went to working men's clubs and public houses. I was well looked after though. There were two little boys aged about seven and nine fostered opposite who were not allowed indoors, and they sat on the front doorstep in all weathers. One was traumatised for life by the experience.'

Colin Bishop was evacuated from Brighton on 29 May 1941, a date he remembers well because it was his birthday. His mother had gone to work as usual, leaving his older sister Norah in charge of him. Very early, she told him to get up as he was about to undertake 'a big journey'. Colin gives a vivid account of how the day took shape:

> My sister gave me my breakfast and saw that I washed and dressed myself: she was doing as my Mum had told her. There I was, all ready to go, but I didn't know where. I had a small suitcase and the only two toys I owned. I had to meet my Mum outside the factory where she worked. She came out of the works gate, gave me a smile and off we went to Brighton railway station. I had never been there before. There were two ladies waiting for us and about thirty children. We said our good-byes, went through the iron gates on to the platform, and there was the train that would take us to the last stop before the moon. We boarded the train, waved good-bye to our mums and then we were on our way. It was around 10am. The only food we had was what we had brought with us and that was going to have to last us all day. And it did take all day to get to where we were heading, but no one would tell us where that was.

The day dragged on and when it got dark, because of the black-out, there were no lights to indicate whether they were going through towns or countryside. At long last one of the ladies announced that the next stop would be theirs, so the children got their things together and waited for the train to stop. They dismounted and stood in a line on the station platform, where two men were waiting to usher them on to a 'single-decker bus' that stood outside. 'No one said a word,' explains Colin. 'We all wondered what was going to happen to us, and we did not have long to wait.' When the bus stopped the names of two little girls were called out, and they were taken off. The bus moved on again, repeating the process until eventually Colin's own name was called. He was dropped off alone and was to stay with a lady called Mrs Jolly who had no children, so he was going to be on his own. 'The only kind words that one of the men said as a parting shot was, "Be at the school in the morning."'

It was now late, so Colin was put to bed for what he describes as 'a nightmare sleep'. The wooden camp bed with a canvas sheet stretched over it creaked and groaned with every move. From then on he chose to sleep on the floor. In the morning Mrs Jolly called him, provided a 'good' breakfast and got him ready for his walk to school, explaining that he would come home for his midday meal. 'I walked out into the street and had a look around,' says Colin. 'I saw a boy of my own age who lived in the house opposite and said "Hello, could you help me to get to the school." "Yes," was the answer so I crossed over the street.' Colin and the boy would remain friends for the next three years. His name was Percy and he showed Colin a short cut down his father's garden path, over the fence, and across a field, a route that would become very familiar over time.

Having arrived at Thurcroft Modern School, in the village of Thurcroft in Yorkshire, Colin was reunited with all the girls and boys from Brighton who had travelled up with him the day before. They were comforted by the sight of two of their own teachers who had arrived before them, who showed them to their classrooms. Being 11, Colin was put into the senior class. Initially all the Brighton kids were kept together, but after the summer holidays they were integrated with the local children.

Not long after arriving Colin was told to report to Mr Elphick, one of the teachers who had come up with them from Brighton. He was informed that Mrs Jolly wanted him out of her house and he was going to be re-billeted. He never knew the reason for this, or what he had done wrong, but the move proved fortuitous as he went to the home of a couple called Mr and Mrs Mosely who were much kinder to him, and who provided him with a real bed to sleep in.

Colin enjoyed his time in Yorkshire, especially working in the school allotments, the produce of which was sold from a shed on Saturdays. At 14 years of age, in the summer of 1944, he left school and, after working for a while at a public house in Thurcroft, bade farewell to his foster parents and returned to his home on the south coast.

In some instances, children ran the risk of becoming too attached to their surrogate wartime parents, and vice versa. Such was the case with Auntie May, who fostered Barbara Wood. Barbara's situation could have been very different had fate taken another course. Her uncle lived in Detroit in the USA, and the initial plan was to send Barbara and her sister Lily to live with his family for the duration of the war. The sisters were taken to the school clinic for medical examinations, and to the dentist to have six perfectly good teeth removed, but as their departure drew near, their parents had a change of heart and decided instead, in March 1941, to send them to Yorkshire with other evacuated children from Brighton. They travelled by train to Ripon and Barbara's most vivid memory of the journey is sharing the contents of her lunch box with other children. She and Lily had raw carrots among their goodies and these proved very popular with their fellow travellers, enabling them to make some tasty swaps. In Ripon they boarded a coach bound for a village called Grewelthorpe, where a teacher took Lily and Barbara by the hands and walked them to the nearby home of the couple who would become known to them as Auntie May and Uncle Albert:

> I remember our first outing with Auntie May was to the village church grave-yard, to visit her daughter Jean's grave who had died at the age of ten months. I have very strong memories of feeling incredibly homesick but do not remember crying. Lily, who is nineteen months older than me, was also missing Mum and Dad. I was a nervous and shy child and had developed a dependency on my big sister, who was more confident and outgoing. A very strong bond developed between us as we struggled to cope with our loss and the challenges ahead. I know I would not have coped without my sister at my side, cuddling each other at night. I was reluctant to let her out of my sight.

Auntie May and Uncle Albert gave them a safe and happy home, and Barbara appreciates how difficult it must have been, especially for Auntie May, to cope with the two young girls. She had a particular problem with bed wetting and explains how understanding Auntie May was, even on the occasion when Lily and Barbara decided to dry the wet bed by placing a library book between the sheets to allow air in. In the morning imagine their horror at finding the sheets stained red.

> Grewelthorpe was a small village, really just one street. Our house was beside the pond and the back gate opened into a field where cows were grazed. On one occasion we opened the gate to find a bull in the field and refused to move through mud to Auntie May's admonishments and amusement. The school had just two classrooms, one for the under-sevens which I was in, and the other for seven to elevens, which Lily was in. During the lunch breaks selected children were lined up and each in turn given a teaspoon of cod liver oil. Lily escaped this but being of slight build I was not so lucky. We attended church where Lily and I enjoyed being allowed to pump the organ.

108 *Barbara Wood (left) and her sister Lily in 1941, during their evacuation to Grewelthorpe in Yorkshire.*

For some, evacuation was an experience associated with abuse and feelings of loneliness and loss, but for others, like Barbara and Lily, it could be a wonderful adventure. Uncle Albert's parents had a farm at the other end of the village that they would often visit. On one occasion Uncle Albert was helping his father ring the snouts of his pigs. This was done inside a barn, the pigs secured by a rope which passed over a door. Lily and Barbara were asked to hold it tight and on no account let go. 'Good fun, we thought,' explains Barbara, 'until the pig squealed and we both let go of the rope and ran away. Uncle Albert was not pleased.'

Haymaking was another time of fun on the farm. Auntie May drove the tractor, and the hay was forked up on to the trailer pulled behind. The girls were allowed to sit on top of the trailer load of hay for the ride back to the barn. 'We also enjoyed sliding down the hay chute,' she muses, 'until we got splinters in our bottoms.' They visited Auntie May's mother, Mrs Crossley, who lived beside the railway line and would welcome them to her home with a cuddle on her lap. The girls also called at the signal box where the signalman would tell them stories. He also played a gramophone record, at their constant request, on which men could be heard swearing. When Auntie May found out about it she forbade the man from playing it any more.

Opposite the farm was a wood where the girls would go exploring. In the early mornings Uncle Albert would go there to shoot rabbits, which his dog Brenda would retrieve. The girls were never allowed to go with him on these excursions, and Brenda was a working dog and lived in a kennel in the backyard, so was never looked on as a family pet. The girls did have pet rabbits and after school they would wander the fields and lanes to pick their food Auntie May making certain they undertook this task every day.

At the end of July the girls were informed that their parents were coming to stay with them for a week. On the day of their arrival Lily and Barbara sat in the front garden shelling peas in eager anticipation. At last a taxi pulled up and out stepped their parents. Although they were pleased to see them, there were no hugs and kisses. The house only had two bedrooms, so the four of them shared the double bed, the girls had been sleeping in. The week sped by and their parents returned home to Brighton.

Every week without fail since their evacuation, their mother had sent them a parcel which they would excitedly open. On 22 August it was Barbara's seventh birthday and an extra large parcel arrived containing a black doll. It was about this time that Barbara became unwell but nobody, including the doctor, could find anything physically wrong with her. 'Now I wonder,' she contemplates, 'if there was a case of homesickness.' In September their parcel contained a letter announcing that mother would be coming to take them home. Auntie May and Lily were terribly upset, but Barbara recalls an enormous sense of relief. On the day their mother was supposed to fetch them, the girls were woken by a disturbance in their room. Auntie Hilda had come up from Brighton instead of mother, and she and Auntie May were feverishly packing their few belongings. Barbara and Lily later learnt that their mother felt unable to face taking the girls away from Auntie May, who in turn could not face a protracted goodbye so requested they left the next morning. Barbara concludes:

109   *Barbara and Lily with Auntie May and another evacuee called Jean from Leeds, who was staying with a neighbour.*

110   *Barbara and Lily pictured with Mrs Crossley, Auntie May's mother who lived beside the railway line.*

111   *Barbara and Lily, with their mother and father visiting them in Yorkshire, and Auntie May behind.*

Auntie May walked with us the one mile across the fields to the nearest bus stop in the next village to catch the 7am bus. Here we said our good-byes. We arrived back in Brighton mid-afternoon and I raced into the house eager to rush into Mum's arms. Where was she? I went into the garden and there she was sitting on the wall. 'Hello Moom' and she burst into tears. A momentary panic: perhaps she didn't want us home! The emotions passed and the family was reunited and at peace, happy at being together again. To Mum's relief, in time we lost our Yorkshire accents.

112   *Lily and Barbara in the front, with Auntie May, Mrs Crossley, and their mother in the back, in a deserted building in the woods around Grewelthorpe.*

113   *Lily and Barbara with their mother, during her trip to visit them in Grewelthorpe.*

While children were away, their parents would invariably worry about them. In order to minimise their concerns, it seems that a sort of censorship was introduced, with regard to the letters the children were permitted to send home. Vena Bartlett was evacuated to Exeter from her home in Rosyth:

At first I settled down well enough, but it gradually came about that I became an outsider, receiving less and less as time went on. I was hungry and miserable and very, very homesick for my dear Mum and Dad. As my letters home were always censored they were entirely unaware of my plight and I could think of no way to let them know. Until, that is, the evening when I had written my weekly letter and had it inspected by my new guardian and a providential knock at the front door took her out of the sitting room. Providence also arranged that she had got as far as folding the letter and putting it in the envelope, which was not yet stuck down. With the quickness born out of desperation, I tore a small fragment of paper from a book and scribbled 'I hate it here,' and poked it into the envelope, seconds before she returned. I was terrified that she might forget she had read the letter or that the scrap might drop out on to the carpet before sticking down the envelope, but luck was with me and I breathed again. It says much for the Royal Mail, especially in wartime, that the letter was posted that evening and the very next day my loving father was standing on the doorstep. There were no recriminations; he simply said that my mother was missing me and so he had come to take me home. Laughing and crying, I shoved my clothes into a suitcase, said 'Thank you' (at Dad's instigation) and 'Goodbye' to my hostess, and together we sped hand in hand to the station. Years later I learned that when Mum had opened the letter the little piece of paper had fluttered to the floor. Picking it up and reading 'I hate it here' caused her to scream 'GO AND GET THAT CHILD AT ONCE, HAROLD!'

A Clash of Cultures

How did this influx of strange beings from another world impact on the lives of those who lived in the countryside? Ten-year-old Allan Thomas lived in Helston, to where children were evacuated from London. His mother took in a boy and a girl who spoke with broad Cockney accents while he admits to having a very broad Cornish accent, but as his mother had lived in London for some time before the war, she quickly got to terms with their jargon and was able to translate what was being said, until the children got used to each others very different regional dialects. Allan was a pupil at Helston Grammar School, and the children sent to live among them were pupils of West Ham Grammar School. The buildings did not have the facilities to educate all these children at once, so the local kids attended school in the mornings, and the visitors used the premises in the afternoons.

The City of Worcester Grammar School for Girls opened its doors to many new pupils, including a large detachment of evacuees from King Edward's School for Girls in Birmingham. Betty Howat was a pupil at the former school and explains that local girls were taught in the morning between 8.30am and 1pm, while the Birmingham girls had the place from 1.30pm until 6pm. There was only ever time for one games lesson a week, which was either tennis, netball or hockey. Betty's husband Andrew lived in Altrincham in Cheshire, and his school opened its doors to evacuees from Manchester, most of whom were found billets in local homes. 'With the

114   *A class of infants evacuated from New Malden in London are having lessons around the dining room table of a home in a safe area.*

influx of new children,' he confirms, 'schools were under pressure and part-time education was introduced. I attended from 9am to 1pm.'

Huggate in Yorkshire was a sparsely populated area where early in the war little seemed to happen, apart from the construction of a nearby army camp. The village school had two teachers and some 36 pupils. John Hoggard was fortunate in having only about a quarter of a mile to walk to school. Children on outlying farms had to walk some two or three miles each way in all kinds of weather. No transport was provided and families had no means of driving their children to school as they do today. Heating in the school was provided by a coke stove and pupils carried the coke from a store to replenish the fire. Snow often blocked the roads on the Yorkshire Wolds and fuel could not be delivered. This meant school had to close for a time, much to the delight of the children. Then evacuees arrived in the village from Sunderland and Hull, along with their teachers, and seemed strange to the villagers as they had very different dialects and appearances. Not all of them fitted in and most returned to their own homes after a few months.

At Tasburgh in Norfolk, William Moore's aunt, like most other villagers, took in evacuees, a mother and son from London. They had been in the house less than two weeks when one morning both had vanished with cash and other small valuables. The police soon picked them up. Being Londoners they thought they could make a quick getaway, but had not banked on the fact that rural areas had relatively poor public transport.

115 *Girls of Notre Dame High School, Liverpool, who were evacuated to Wales, preparing for a game of hockey.*

Bill Underwood and his evacuee friend Mervyn were also picked up by the police, but this was due to a misunderstanding. 'During the summer of 1942,' Bill explains, 'I was thirteen years of age. My friend Mervyn Collett, the evacuee from Sheffield, and myself, decided one Sunday to hitchhike to Silbury Hill. We set off after lunch and walked about three and a half miles before we got our first lift. It was a police car who thought we were evacuees running away. They delivered us back to our homes and told us not to try it again.'

At Cayton in Yorkshire, Jenny Peacock notes that most of the refugees who came to the Scarborough area were from Hull. Being from the city they were ignorant about the countryside, and 'a lot didn't even know that eggs came from chickens or milk from cows,' she explains. Children in the cities were provided with powdered eggs and powdered milk, so many of them would not have seen a real egg for quite a while, if at all.

At Great Clifton, the arrival of one particular evacuee had a very positive affect on Ken Carruthers. Having received an appeal for volunteers to foster children, his mother went along to the infants school and returned with 'a little sister'. The girl's name was Margaret Fenwick and she was six years old and from South Shields. 'My own little sister Hilda died as a baby,' states Ken, 'so I never knew her.' Margaret had two sisters, one elsewhere in the village and another somewhere different. But the evacuee in question was billeted in the house opposite and her carer asked Ken if he would befriend her. 'She was about ten years old,' explains Ken, 'and, believe me, she was the first love of my life. We were never parted until the day my heart was broken, when she had to go back home to South Shields. Her name was Marjorie Tobias, and I still think of her today. My first taste of puppy love.'

Ethel Fisher attended Flimby Girls School and during the latter part of 1939 they received an influx of evacuees from South Shields and Newcastle upon Tyne. The girls from both schools were initially 'squashed' into the same classroom. Ethel describes how school life changed quite dramatically. For instance, they were not allowed to use pen and ink and had to write everything in pencil because paper was in very short supply and had to be stretched between the pupils of two schools. So every Friday afternoon the girls spent the last period of the day erasing all the work they had done in their exercise books during the week in order to be able to use the same paper again the following week. Books usually lasted about a month before being classed as 'rubbed to

116 *Ken Carruthers with evacuee Margaret Fenwick from South Shields, who stayed at his home in Cumbria for eighteen months. Also in the picture is Ken's little cousin John Bell.*

death', and new ones were issued. 'We had four prefects in the top class,' says Ethel. 'Two of them spent the last ten minutes of every day searching through the waste paper baskets in every classroom, and if they found any paper fit to be written on the teacher from that particular classroom had to report to the headmistress and give an explanation as to why.'

Rosa Bowler's memories are not so much of the children who were evacuated as their teachers: Miss Parry, a tall business-like lady who taught general subjects, and Miss McDougall, a large round-faced woman with glasses and brown hair fastened in a bun who taught needlework. They both came from London. Miss McDougall always wore bottle-green clothes and lodged with Rosa's Auntie Marn. Local children and London evacuees made around seventy pupils at Ilsley school, far too many for the classrooms to cope with, so some children were taught in the passageway.

Water was very precious as it had to be brought into the house in buckets, so it was common for people to share their bath water. One evening, Auntie Marn was sharing the 'big old iron bath' with Rosa's mother when the air-raid siren sounded. The two panicked and fell about in the darkness of the black-out. Miss Parry and Miss McDougall were sitting downstairs at the time and Rosa remembers them being quite shocked when: 'Mum and Marnie came flying down the stairs, black and blue from where they had knocked one another over in their scramble to get out of the bath. They were both stark naked.'

Rosa also remembers a London evacuee called Joan who came to stay. She was 11 years old and had very short black hair and no teeth, presumably as a result of a poor diet. The younger Rosa was used to being the centre of attention so did not take kindly to this intrusion, especially when she had to fight for the affections of her own grandfather. She admits to not being very nice to the poor girl and one day bit her quite severely. Her grandfather promptly took hold of Rosa's hand and bit it in return. She cried profusely but a lesson was learnt and in time she grew to accept the newcomer.

In the Pembrokeshire village of Porthgain the council took over a large empty house near the farm on which Mr Charles lived. Three families evacuated from London were housed here and one of them was the Harold family, consisting of two boys, one girl and their mother. The boys were Jimmy aged 16 and George aged fourteen. With the shortage of farm labourers, Mr Charles's father, who was highly regarded for his ability to teach young boys in farming methods, decided to employ the two brothers. He taught George to drive a horse and cart, and the boy became obsessed with his ability to

117   *Rosa Bowler (centre) in her garden at East Ilsley, with her mother and their London evacuee Joan.*

handle them. Every load of corn he brought in from the fields at harvest time was something to celebrate. His obsession turned fantastical and he would sometimes relate the most incredible stories to illustrate his affinity with horses. Mr Charles particularly remembers the tale of the runaway horse galloping through the streets of London. According to George, no one in the city, including the police, was able to stop it, until he appeared on the scene. 'He leapt up,' Mr Charles recounts, 'caught the horse's mane and hung on to its neck until he was able to grab the reins and bring it to a halt. Of course, we all knew the stories were not true but we always listened and responded to them as if they were.' Another amusing story concerns to a seven-year-old evacuee girl who Mr Charles explains was staying at a friend's house, where she fell head over heels in love with the 17-year-old son of her new foster parents. Everybody, including Mr Charles, teased the teenager about his admirer, who took it all very well. One day he heard the little girl approach her 'true love' with the following plea: 'Yesterday you were with Betty, today you are with Jenny. Tomorrow perhaps you will be with me?'

A strong bond still unites many people with the children who came to stay under such unique circumstances. They have kept in touch, or sought to reunite themselves with their wartime brothers and sisters. Jean Pearse was only three when the war began and recalls how a nursery school was set up in the village of Holbeton where she lived. Both local children and pre-school evacuees from

Acton attended the nursery. One of the evacuees was Georgina Swan who was the same age as Jean. They became friends and started school together. In later life Jean often wondered what had become of her friend, so she decided to find her again and eventually tracked her down to Milton Keynes. When she called at her house, Georgina mistook her for the 'Avon lady', but after recognising the familiar face even after the passing of fifty years, the couple cried and happy memories flooded back.

Safe in the Country

Another form of evacuation that affected many children was privately managed, parents living in cities and towns taking it upon themselves to send their children to relatives in parts of the country away from the bombs. This would have been for varying lengths of time. Some people spent the entire war away from their homes, while others enjoyed the temporary respite of holidays or weekends in the country. BBC radio presenter Malcolm Laycock is known for presenting programmes such as

118   *Malcolm Laycock in Bradford Grammar School blazer c.1950. He spent much of the war in Blackpool.*

'As Time Goes By', and 'Jazz For The Asking'. It might not be a huge surprise to learn that it was forced evacuation from his home in Bradford that brought about his life-long love of music.

> I blame Joe Loss. It was definitely he who got me into this broadcasting and big band mess. How come? Well, I spent much of my wartime youth in Blackpool escaping Bradford's unfounded fear of bombs. As the Music Hall gag goes, if a bomb had fallen on Bradford, it would have done at least two pounds' worth of damage. Accordingly, I was packed off to Blackpool at every opportunity to stay with my Aunt Gertie, a landlady. She lived at South Shore just across the railway lines from the end of the Big Dipper. She weighed over 22 stones – in her stockinged feet. But she was as light as a feather on those feet. When she got into the back of grandpa's car to sit next to grandma, she plopped down with such force that all the air rushed to the other end of the seat and shot grandma up to the roof with a thud. I enjoyed that, but not as much as her malapropisms. She once told me she'd had a new frock made 'with a moffet on it'. For years I wondered what a moffet was, until eventually the penny dropped. She meant a motif. After a speech she gave to the landlady's guild, they presented her with a bucket (bouquet!) of flowers. And when she broke her leg, she had to sit up in the hospital bed with a canopy (caliper!).
>
> It was Aunt Gertie who first taught me to dance in the Tower Ballroom to the Joe Loss Orchestra. You see, Aunt Gertie had no choice but to partner me because Uncle Ted had lost a leg in the trenches in the First World War and kept his wooden one hanging by its leather straps on a peg in the hall. Aunt Gertie always said he was only any good for the one-step, and he would grin at her and nonchalantly flick more cigarette ash on the floor under his chair when she wasn't looking. I once recounted these events to Mildred Loss and said that therefore it was certainly Joe who unwittingly got me into this broadcasting and big band mess. She just giggled.

The fear of bombing in Bradford may have been slightly exaggerated, but in Bristol Doreen Govan was in the thick of it, and in the spring of 1942 her mother decided to send her to the country. 'A very nice billet was found on a farm at Burrington, Somerset,' explains Doreen. 'I spent all the summer holidays and every weekend there, coming back by bus each Monday for school.' Doreen describes her adventures in the Mendip Hills as like being in 'another world'. She loved every minute of it, especially being around farm animals, chickens and ducks. Other evacuees in the village were from London, so there were always other children to share her pleasures. She remembers 'really thick milk which stayed on the inside of your glass when you drank it, and any amount of eggs'. At haymaking time she was allowed to help on the farm and her favourite job was leading the big carthorse up and down the straight lines of cut hay. She loved to feel the warmth of the horse's breath on her hand as she held firmly on to the bit ring. One day at the end of the summer, when she was back home in Bristol, she met the coalman on her way home from school. Flushed with her success with carthorses on the farm,

> I persuaded him to let me drive his cart down the road to deliver coal at the houses. What I had not reckoned on was Mum coming out of the house just as I drew level. Her look of outraged horror was a sight to see. There was

her daughter immaculate in school uniform, blue and white dress, royal blue blazer, Panama hat with the blue band round it, thoroughly enjoying herself, competently holding the reins of a huge carthorse, drawing a coal cart down the road for all to see.

In 1939 Bill Hawkins was eight and lived in Portsmouth with his three older sisters, sick mother, and father who was a Royal Marines pensioner. As soon as the war began his father was recalled to colours and posted to Scapa Flow in the Orkney Islands. His parents chose not to include Bill and their youngest daughter Joan in the original evacuation scheme, but after his mother died in May 1940 and the Blitz on the city began, it was decided to send them away privately to stay with their father's sister and her husband, who owned a small farm on the outskirts of Trowbridge in Wiltshire. Bill was now ten and Joan thirteen. Mr Hawkins explains that although Aunt Olive, a tall, thin, grey-haired lady, was a strict disciplinarian, he loved her dearly. Uncle Reg, 'a true country person', taught him all about birds and animals, and really educated him about English nature. At every opportunity they would walk together along the bank of the nearby River Avon, or on the towpath of the Kennet and Avon Canal, where he absorbed all the wonders around him.

Although there were a few cows and sheep, the main job of the farm was to produce thousands of chickens and eggs, and it felt 'strange and wonderful' to a city boy. Bill and Joan would be called at seven every morning and after breakfast

119   *The wedding of Cyril and Viola Licquorish on 18 September 1943, in the village chapel at Cottingham in Leicestershire. The following day Cyril had to return to barracks. The bridesmaid on the far right is London evacuee Lily, who arrived at Cyril's home in 1942 aged ten. Since the war she kept in touch with Cyril and Viola and even attended their silver, golden and diamond wedding anniversaries.*

of toast and 'fresh' eggs would walk the three miles to school in Trowbridge. They had a friend in the village, Malcolm, another ten-year-old evacuee from London, who would walk to school with them. Malcolm had been billeted on a local family against their wishes and was treated appallingly. While in Bill's company he always seemed to be crying, while at other times and in other company he would put a brave face on things.

As well as running the farm, Uncle Reg had a part-time job driving a 'rattly old lorry' around the country lanes between 8am and 10am collecting churns of fresh cow's milk to take to the Nestles factory. At weekends, or whenever possible, Bill would go with him and says, 'I swear the lorry had solid tyres and no suspension.' He would also be treated to a few ladles of the delicious warm milk straight from the churns. He describes the usual evening meal as being the 'sort that would have delighted and amazed any other family during the war'. They almost always had chicken, and sometimes pork, with fresh vegetables straight from the huge farmhouse garden. Uncle Reg said it was the only 'perk' of being a farmer. Reg and Olive were certainly doing their bit for the war effort, supplying the country with thousands of live chickens and hundreds of thousands of eggs that were collected from the farm weekly by huge lorries. In fact, Bill's only unpleasant memory of life on the farm was having to drink a glass full of cabbage water every evening after dinner. It tasted revolting but Aunt Olive watched to make sure he swallowed every last drop. 'It will make you strong and healthy,' she insisted.

> Regrettably, our idyllic country life lasted barely a year, and by mid-1942 Joan and I returned to Portsmouth. Probably the fact that the city had not had a serious air raid for many months may have had something to do with that decision, but the main reason as far as I knew was that Dad had remarried (how, when and where remains a mystery) and he wanted us back home with his new wife. My new stepmother, Janet, was a very short and dumpy woman measuring about five feet in every direction. What my father saw in her I cannot begin to imagine as he himself was an upright six foot tall Marine.

Bill's first memory of his new stepmother was when he and Joan first arrived back from Trowbridge, very tired and hungry after their long journey.

> We were sat at the table and served with an awful meal of mashed powdered potatoes that tasted like wallpaper paste, and spam slices swamped in a congealed gravy that had dried around the edges where Janet had been 'keeping it warm' for the last few hours. It was terrible and in complete contrast to the fresh food we had enjoyed for the last year. Of course, that was not her fault. Nevertheless, it was not an auspicious start to our relationship that never rose above the level of mutual dislike. I do not doubt that this was mainly my fault. With Dad still being away in Scapa, I was probably an undisciplined, annoying brat, badly in need of strict parental control, but I would willingly have swapped my 'freedom' for a little motherly love, an affection that was certainly not forthcoming from Janet.

Author and illustrator Raymond Briggs, perhaps best known for *The Snowman*, found himself evacuated from London to Dorset, to stay with two aunties:

There I lived with my Auntie Flo and Auntie Betty in a small stone cottage with only three rooms, no bathroom, no electricity, and no inside lavatory. Auntie Betty was very proud of the new cold water tap which was now, for the first time, inside the cottage. The possibility of a German invasion was always in everyone's mind and Aunt Betty, who was the boss, kept three suitcases ready-packed for instant flight. We never had air raids there, as we were in the depths of the countryside, but one night we were woken by a deafening burst of machine gun fire. It was terrifyingly loud and seemed frighteningly close. We all sat up in bed with our hearts thumping. 'Get the cases, Flo!' cried Aunt Betty. We struggled down the curving stone staircase with the suitcases and stood there bewildered and trembling in our dressing gowns. Then came two distant thumps which we heard later were bombs falling harmlessly in fields and causing the face of a grandfather clock in the farmhouse to fall out. Quite where we were going, two elderly ladies and a five-year-old boy, in the middle of the night, with no car and not even a pram or wheelbarrow to push, I never discovered.

After only one month of war Molly Kinghorn and her sister were evacuated from Leeds, Joan to an aunt at Sicklinghall near Wetherby and Molly to Pannal Ash near Harrogate, where her uncle managed a dairy farm. He had two Land Army girls allocated to work for him and Molly says that to this day she fancies herself in a green jumper with khaki bib and brace. The two girls couldn't have been more different. Mary was a typical country girl who could turn her hand to any job, while Naomi, was a doctor's daughter who had never seen a farm in her life, except in pictures. She hated getting her hands dirty and it was some time before she could bring herself to touch the cows udders for milking. Molly's aunt made butter and sold cream, but now she could only sell butter to registered customers, and to do this she also had to sell margarine and lard as well.

Molly found the change of school a bit strange, especially the headmaster who inspected the children every morning to check they had clean hands and nails. He also examined their handkerchiefs and shoes, to make sure they were polished. On the walk home Molly and

120   *Raymond Briggs, who as a five year old found himself living in rural Dorset with two aunts.*

her friends would often meet airmen being marched back to their billets at Pannal Ash and Ashville Colleges, which had given up their peacetime roles as boarding schools. A friendly sergeant allowed the children to fall in and march home with them. One day, as they were out in the playground, a man riding by on a bicycle shouted at them to go inside and get under their desks as there was a German plane overhead. Molly did not believe him because no sirens had sounded and, there was a siren on the wall of the school, but the man's story was perfectly correct. A German plane had just flown over Harrogate firing guns into the centre of town. Leeds it transpired, was no more dangerous than Harrogate, so it was decided that Molly should return home again.

Gerald Hamer's initial evacuation took a very different course, away from the relative quiet of South Wales to the hustle and bustle of Birmingham, a sort of evacuation in reverse. His father was a coal miner and the family lived in Tredegar, but work was so scarce they chose to move. His two elder brothers moved first and succeeded in getting both jobs and a house to rent, so the rest of the family joined them in Smethwick. But then the bombing started, and Gerald's mother wanted to get him and his brother out of the city. It all came to a head when a German bomber dropped a landmine right outside the house. Fortunately it floated down on a parachute that hooked itself on a telegraph pole but the street was evacuated while it was removed. The incident prompted his mother to get her sons added to the evacuation list. Gerald had a sister who was three years younger, but his mother decided she was too young to be parted from her.

Gerald and his brother were sent to Wellington near Telford, but the landlady with whom they were billeted did not treat them very well so their mother took

121 *Joan Bennet came to Yorkshire as a teenage evacuee and was adopted by Molly Kinghorn's Auntie Dora, whose husband was head gardener at a country estate called Moor Park Hall. She subsequently met and married RAF navigator, John Tweed.*

122   *A tragic wartime family. Baby Eileen Littlechild pictured with her mother and father in Plymouth in 1940. Also present are her sister Margaret and brother Arthur. Her mother died shortly after the photograph was taken and the other (younger) sister in the photograph died later. Eileen grew up thinking she was an only child, but 67 years later Margaret and Arthur finally tracked down their lost sister.*

them back to Birmingham. The bombing was getting so intense that desperate measures were required and their father wrote to a brother living in Welwyn Garden City in Hertfordshire. This resulted in Gerald, his mother and sister being offered a room until they were able to rent a house of their own while his father and brothers remained in Birmingham. In time, the family was given one of a group of houses that had been used by the army during the build up to the invasion of Europe. The floorboards were covered with indentations left by heavy hob-nailed boots. Out in the garden the soldiers had dug a 'zig zag trench' in which to practise for the coming campaign. The new residents filled this in and, under the piles of soil the soldiers had left, found a pickaxe and a shovel. The house, built out of breeze blocks, was very basic, but Mr Hamer explains that after so many moves they were at last happy.

With so many children moving around the country, it was inevitable that some would get lost in the system. One moving story is told by Jean Pearse, who lived in the village of Holbeton near Plymouth. Her daughter's mother-in-law once told her she had no idea who her own family was, where they lived, or what became of them. She was born in a Plymouth hospital in 1940 and her birth certificate named her as Eileen Littlechild, even though everybody knew her as Joan. As a baby Joan had been fostered by a family in Holbeton, and when she was five she was adopted by a couple in Salcombe. As far as she was aware she had no blood relations.

In 2007 Jean noticed an appeal in the local paper: 'Where are they now, Eileen Littlechild born in the war in Plymouth 67 years ago.' She recognised the name immediately, and when Joan visited the house later that day showed her the appeal. Joan burst into tears to think that somebody was looking for her, rang the number printed in the paper and left her details. A week later the phone rang and a lady's voice announced that she was her sister Margaret who was living in Essex. She also had a brother living in Waterlooville near Portsmouth. Jean explains:

> Joan's brother and sister had been evacuated down to Redruth in Cornwall, but they always remembered their mother having a baby girl and that their mother had died in Plymouth in the war. Joan found that she had nieces, nephews and cousins. And, of course, Joan's own son and daughter also had cousins of their own for the first time. Joan's family had been looking for many years. September last year they all had a big reunion. I myself was lucky enough to meet Arthur Littlechild when he came to Devon to thank me for finding his sister.

I wonder how many more children were lost at this time, separated from their parents through evacuation, never finding their way home again? Evacuation helped to keep many children out of danger but they were forced to live in unfamiliar homes, to live with people they did not know. They were often subjected to abuse while at their most vulnerable. For some people evacuation was a happy experience, but for others it was a waking nightmare.

Chapter 8

Britain under Attack

Although there were numerous attacks on military targets in the first few months of the war, the general public came through relatively unscathed. This was the lull before the storm, as before long the skies over southern Britain became a daily battlefield. One of the clearest memories that children have of the Second World War is the Battle of Britain. In the summer of 1940 Britain stood alone and for children all over the south there was a daily spectacle of dogfights in the sky. The official Battle of Britain period lasted from 10 July 1940 to 31 October 1940. During this time there was the start of a more menacing period known as the Blitz, the long anticipated attack on civilian targets. Although the bombing of London began on 23 August 1940, the heavy raids didn't commence until 7 September, and from then until the end of the war children in many parts of Britain found themselves in mortal danger.

The Bombing of London

The Blitz on London was the most ferocious and concerted attack that Britain has ever been subjected to. Night after night, waves of between two and four hundred bombers would drop high explosives all over the city. At one point this happened on 57 consecutive nights. The aim of the Luftwaffe was to destroy London's infrastructure in one knockout blow by targeting power stations, docks, railways and aerodromes. They also attacked civilian suburbs on an unprecedented scale. Their hope was to destroy the city's ability to function, and to demoralise the British people so much that their government would be forced to capitulate.

At the height of the Blitz, between September 1940 and May 1941, over 50,000 high explosive bombs were dropped on London, as well as tens of thousands of incendiary bombs. 1,150,000 houses were damaged and over 1,400,000 people were made homeless. In total, over 41,000 British civilians were killed during the war, and 137,000 injured. Of the dead, 7,736 were children. Thousands of children escaped the Blitz thanks to the evacuation scheme, but many more remember living in the capital through the troubled times. Among them was a young boy called Michael Winner, who became one of Britain's most celebrated film producers. What are his memories of this traumatic period?

> I particularly remember watching the traffic lights going from red to green via orange. It was wartime and they were the only lights you could see from the window of our flat near Hyde Park. Then there would be the sound of the air-raid sirens. Then the drone of aeroplanes in the sky. This would be followed by

the most wonderful and spectacular display, which to a five-year-old child was pure delight. The anti-aircraft guns a few yards away in the park would start to fire. The searchlights that rested among them would pierce the sky with their beams of light occasionally hitting upon enemy aircraft. The barrage balloons which rose up like floating, fat fish would be illuminated from time to time by the searchlights. There would be the whistle of bombs, explosions and the sight of distant fires. Of course, these were terrible things. But to a child interested in unusual visions, it was like an extraordinary theatrical event.

123   *In this painting by Joe Crowfoot, children watch as Spitfires cross the Channel coast of England.*

Diana Bewers was 11 at the time of the London Blitz. She lived above her father's shop in Banstead, Surrey, an area which suffered from being on the flightpath of German incursions. She spent many nights in a little room behind the shop under the stairs. Her father had fashioned her a bunk bed while he and his wife slept on a mattress on the floor. From this sanctuary they could hear the bombers passing overhead, night after night, and sometimes Banstead would be bombed when the planes returning from London ejected any cargo that remained in their holds. 'We were particularly worried about incendiary bombs,' Diana recalls, 'as my father had a yard full of paraffin tanks to supply small holders and other local people.'

One night, as her father checked his yard, he noticed a red glow in the sky to the north. He went up to the top bedroom and called down to his wife and daughter to come up and look. 'The whole sky was lit up over London,' writes Diana. 'The fires seemed to cover a large area. We were 14 miles from the city but the sight was terrifying. We went back to bed and thought of my mother's brother who was in the fire service. We were pretty sure he would be attending a fire as big as that.' After another day and night her uncle appeared, black and exhausted. He had been fighting fires in the docks without a break since they started, so after a bath and a meal he went to bed. That night Banstead itself was subjected to a very heavy raid. The churchyard was hit and there were gravestones all over the High Street. 'I was not allowed out,' Diana recollects, suspecting that there were bodies in the street that her parents did not wish her to see. The one thing she does remember is that her exhausted uncle slept soundly through the entire event.

Michael Winner describes how, later on in the war, London was again subjected to a new wave of bombing by the V1 flying bomb, which became known as the doodlebug, and the V2 rocket. The V1 was a pilotless aircraft packed with explosives that was launched from ramps on the continent. It had a random target area of around 15 miles and was used with great effect to terrorise the people of

London. The V2 rocket had a range of approximately 200 miles, carried a ton of explosives in its warhead and travelled at around 4,000 miles an hour. It could reach its target within minutes of launch, making the Allies helpless to guard against it. Mr Winner recalls the eerie silence as the V1s stopped in mid-air and the whoosh and scream as they came to ground followed by a muffled explosion. But his most powerful memories are of the people of London themselves and how they coped under such stressful conditions.

> The feeling of togetherness and total commitment that this country had during the war left an indelible memory on those who lived through it. We had a purpose, we were going to win, and the world was going to be a better place. We did win, technically. Whether the world became a better place is a matter of opinion.

Another young boy who survived the London bombing and would go on to achieve theatrical success is the actor Colin Skipp, perhaps best known for his role as Tony Archer is Radio 4's long-running serial *The Archers*. He was only a baby when a doodlebug nearly cut short his life:

124   *The King and Queen visit the people of the East End to express their sympathy after a savage raid. Even here, among the bombed houses, a Union Jack flutters from a window.*

I couldn't have been more than two years of age; my mother was pushing me home in my pram. We'd been shopping and the bags were in the pram with me. We heard the noise of a doodlebug, droning on, carrying its message of hate. Suddenly the noise stopped and my mother snatched me from the pram and hurled me into a garden, then fell on top of me. We were sheltered by a wall and hedge when the explosion happened. We lay in the garden for about five minutes, then got up and started for home. As we rounded the corner of the street where we lived, we could see quite a bit of bomb blast damage. The windows of our house were smashed and we were told that the bomb had dropped about a quarter of a mile away, on an ARP camp: I think there were several air raid policemen dead … this, then, the beginning of my childhood.

Peter Richards became a St John Ambulance cadet and often gave a hand at the North Middlesex Hospital. One night in May 1944, when he was 16, a stick of bombs was dropped on the hospital during one of the final raids on the city. One bomb hit the receiving ward, killing the duty sister, Sister Loftus, and an incendiary bomb destroyed her room in the nurses' house prompting staff to comment 'Her name was really and truly on that bomb!' Some of the men's wards were also damaged, along with the children's ward, where half a dozen boys and girls were recovering from tonsils or adenoids operations. The children's ward was a temporary structure built during the First World War and intended only to last

125 *Women and children bombed out of their London homes find temporary shelter while new accommodation is arranged.*

for around five years. It took a bomb in another war, 25 years later, finally to demolish it. The hospital had its own fire engines but the blast had pushed a heavy door on to the appliances so they could not be used. Peter was also an ARP messenger, so he was sent to a factory next door in order to borrow their fire appliances.

While making his way back to the hospital he discovered a man who was badly shaken by the incident although not physically injured. Peter noticed the front door of a nearby house was open so, assuming an authoritative voice, he more or less demanded that the man be taken inside. Sending him to the hospital would have been pointless. Peter then set about rescuing the children from the bombed ward. They had to be taken to another hospital and Green Line coaches adapted as ambulances were used to ferry them to Bishop's Stortford. 'We must have been in a hurry,' Peter points out, 'as we overtook an American army convoy

126   *Bomb crater outside a London home. The only damage to the house itself, was broken windows and displaced tiles.*

on the way.' There were five cadets on duty that night, two of whom were killed. The surviving three were awarded Bronze Life-Saving Medals of the Order of St John of Jerusalem. In the autumn, Peter and the other two went to St John's Gate, the headquarters of the Order, and were duly presented with their medals by the Duke of Gloucester. 'I was the last on the list,' he proudly states. For his services during the war he was also awarded the Defence Medal.

'I sat my General School Certificate examinations, the equivalent of today's GCSEs, in June 1944 with a tin helmet under my desk,' continues Peter. 'We used the gymnasium as an examination room. Three times during a maths examination I went under my desk for protection; I passed with a credit.' The same thing happened during the Latin exam, which unfortunately he failed.

The school Peter attended had a first aid team of which he was appointed leader. In May 1945 a V2 rocket landed on the school during the lunch hour. Had it landed 20 yards short of where it did, it might have killed several hundred boys sitting down to dinner. As it was, two boys were killed who had left the dining hall prematurely. Another boy lost an arm and one of the masters received superficial cuts to his face from flying glass. One of the few mistresses at the school, there to free up male teachers for the forces, went to administer first aid and promptly fainted into the arms of a prefect. Peter was having lunch at home as he lived quite close to the

127 *Women and children collect a few possessions from their bombed homes after a raid on west London.*

school but, on hearing the commotion and seeing the smoke from where the rocket had made impact, he immediately ran back to give assistance. He helped load one of the injured boys on to an ambulance and saw him die in the process. 'I was at the feet end,' he explains. 'His head, where he had fractured his neck, just flopped and broke his spinal cord.' Peter suggests that had his head been supported by sandbags he might just have lived, but there were no sophisticated head and neck splints in those days. One of the school's governors was an architect and he designed a small monument to the occasion, which stood in the school grounds, but now stands in the grounds of All Saints College, part of Middlesex University.

Some people have bizarre memories of the Blitz. Winifred Taylor recalls sitting on a kerb in Freemasons Road, outside a burning shoe shop trying on shoes. The docks were red with flames and the light from the fires seemed to turn night into day. On another occasion she stood on top of the Anderson shelter watching a German aircraft caught in the searchlight beams. Tracer fire hammered into it until it was finally shot down and the lights followed it as it spiralled to the ground. The next day her family was told by the ARP that the aircraft had crashed on to the maternity wing of Poplar Hospital.

'Opposite where we lived in Ethel Road was an air-raid shelter in the church grounds,' she relates. 'I was in there during an air raid when someone came in shouting that the ARP centre had been hit. I recall a girl screaming "My Dad! My Dad!" She was in the shelter because her family also lived in Ethel Road. I also recall watching the ARP digging people out of their devastated homes. I lost a friend when her home was bombed. I saw her body covered in dust lying on the ground, after she had just been dug out.'

Joyce Caskey was seven years old on the first Saturday of the Blitz. She lived close to the Victoria and Albert Docks and recalls that the raids lasted all day and night. The sky was ablaze and her own house was bombed. Along with others in the street, her family was evacuated to a local school in Agate Street, where around 200 homeless people gathered. They were informed that coaches were coming to take them to safety. They were then given mattresses and settled down to try and sleep on the floor. 'My father was at work in the docks,' she explains, 'and he eventually found where we were. People were running around looking for their family and friends. My mother, my sister and myself lay down on the mattresses to try to get some rest. My mother was feeling unwell, and it was impossible to

128 *The King and Queen sympathise with a young boy who has lost his home during a visit to the bombed London streets on 27 September 1940.*

sleep because the noise of the bombing was horrendous. My father insisted that we leave the school to find another shelter. There was nowhere, only the brick shelter that had been built in the playground for the school children. We just managed to squeeze inside, but were packed in like sardines.' Joyce had a lucky escape as the school later received a direct hit by a land mine. Her two sisters-in-law who had remained behind were among the many killed, their bodies never being found. The coaches finally arrived to rescue the survivors and Joyce remembers emerging into a cold September dawn and being given a blanket to put around her shoulders. 'In that era,' she continues, 'when you had a new doll it always came in a plain cardboard box.' As they waited to board the coaches, she remembers wondering 'where so many boxes of dolls came from' as, unbeknown to her, bodies were being brought out of the rubble.

In January 1944 Margaret Thipthorpe was also seven years old and living in the basement of an aunt's house opposite the Woolwich Dockyard in south-east London. Her mother had been saving food coupons for some months in order to make the first birthday cake she would ever have. This was duly done and it was put on a table ready for her to cut the following day. 'It looked beautiful and I was very excited,' she says. At around midnight, they were woken by the sound of the sirens going off, so they dutifully trooped out to the garden and settled down in the shelter for the night. There was an almighty bang, which must have been a bomb landing quite near, but they were all OK so thought no more of it. Her mother made them a cup of tea and they went back to sleep. In the morning a sorry sight

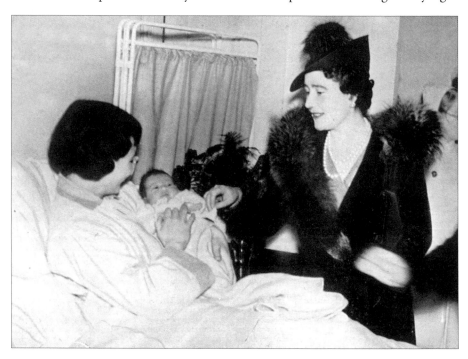

129 *Her Majesty The Queen on one of her many visits to London hospitals attempting to attract the attention of a baby while its happy mother looks on.*

met their eyes. The bomb had landed a little way down the road, but the blast had blown a wall over, right on top of Margaret's lovely cake. 'I don't remember Mum baking anything else,' Margaret states, 'until she made the sausage rolls for our street party when the war ended.'

Targetting the Provinces

The nightly bombing of Britain was not confined to London but aimed at the systematic destruction of major cities and towns, especially those with a heavy industrial base. Southampton, Portsmouth, Plymouth, Bristol, Liverpool, Hull, Coventry, Derby, Leicester, Sheffield, Birmingham, Manchester and Glasgow were among the places badly affected. In Plymouth one household in four was made homeless and on Clydebank, only seven out of twelve thousand homes remained undamaged.

Doreen Govan experienced the first bombing of Bristol on a Sunday evening. It was around six o'clock, and she recalls that tea was over, the curtains were drawn, and she and her parents had settled down to listen to the wireless. No sirens had yet sounded when suddenly her father leapt up, grabbed his wife and daughter, and bundled them into the cupboard under the stairs, throwing himself on top. 'There was an enormous crash somewhere quite nearby,' she explains, 'then the sirens wailed all over the city. Afterwards Mum was to say that Dad went white about the mouth. He had heard the whine of the bomb and recognised the sound from his experiences in the trenches.' After things had quietened down, Doreen and her mother stayed in the cupboard while her father ventured out with the fire-watchers to see what had occurred. Within minutes of the all clear sound their back gate opened, followed by the back door, and her grandfather entered the house covered in what appeared to be soot and plaster. 'I've been hit,' he cryptically announced. On his return, Doreen's father accompanied the man back to his own house to view the damage, armed only with torches. Doreen describes the scene:

> Mrs Shepherd's house next door to Gramps had taken a direct hit and was totally gone. Most of Gramps, house had also gone, including the roof, but the staircase was still intact. When daylight came Mum and I went round to see for ourselves. Poor Mrs Shepherd was out in the road, stumbling through the rubble. She was pulling clothes out of an ottoman and shaking out all the bomb dust and bits of debris. She looked as though she couldn't believe what had happened. When Mum saw what was left of Gramps' house, all she could say was only how thankful she was that Gran hadn't lived to see it. Gran had been rather house-proud and her front room was sacrosanct. There was a huge glass-fronted cabinet full of best glass and china. The three-piece suite was a luxurious plush. Everything was now buried or blown up and covered with smashed glass, rubble and broken beams. Gramps moved in with us for some time.

Among the things that made Bristol a target was the Bristol Aeroplane Company (BAC) at Filton, where hundreds of men and women were employed building war planes on a 24 hour shift system. Doreen believes the day the Luftwaffe caused at havoc the factory was in September 1940, because she had already started at St George Grammar School and during the attack took refuge in the school shelter, while her mother and neighbour Mrs Upton watched the entire event from the garden. Hearing more than the usual number of enemy aircraft, the couple were making their way down to the Anderson shelter, but the sight that met their eyes rooted them to the spot. Wave after wave of bombers passed overhead, all going in the same direction. There were far too many for the fighter aircraft and anti-aircraft guns to deal with. The attack happened around midday, just as the shifts were changing over, so workers were caught out in the open. Many lost their lives, either from the bombs or falling debris, or by being machine-gunned in the open. 'The BAC, though severely damaged, did not close,' states Doreen, 'and the surviving workers returned to carry on making more planes.' The date of the above incident was probably 25 September 1940, when 72 were killed and 166 injured, of whom 19 later died from their injuries. In the area surrounding the factory a further 58 people lost their lives.

Pamela Scott's father was killed at sea and she was evacuated from her Brighton home to Derbyshire. Before going she experienced numerous air raids on the town and saw the two piers have their middles blown out. She recalls that the promenade was 'out of bounds' and covered with barbed wire. 'Brighton', she says, 'became a closed town and you could only go out, or come in, with your identity card. It suffered fairly badly as the enemy planes would sneak along the southern coastal cliffs and then suddenly appear, so there was no time for the sirens.'

Not far away, at Portslade-by-Sea, the mother of John Ayling had a lucky escape when an explosion trapped her in a cupboard. John had been playing in a local park when the town was attacked in broad daylight. He took shelter in a 'wooden structure' outside a shop and clearly remembers the sound of bullets

130   *The Queen talks to children in a Southwark shelter, where bunk beds have been installed.*

131 *The Prime Minister visits bombed Bristol, where he told cheering people, 'We shall give it them back!' The little girl doesn't look very convinced.*

raining down from the machine guns of the low-flying intruders. He eventually arrived home to find the road he lived in was cordoned off. A blast had blown out the windows and doors of his house, and there was a large hole in the roof. His mother had been in the hallway and the blast had thrown her into the cupboard under the stairs, closing the door behind her. She was unhurt and lucky, because the house two doors away had been completely demolished and the residents killed. John's future wife Doreen was seven at the time and living in Coleridge Street, Hove. She recalls standing at the bus stop with friends and teachers one day, when the siren sounded. 'We were looking at each other and wondering where to go,' she recalls, 'when a lady came out of a nearby house and invited us to take cover.'

Another lucky escape in the Brighton area happened on the night of 5 August 1941, when St Cuthman's Church at Whitehawk was demolished. The church was about fifty yards from the home of Elizabeth Gillett, who remembers it being a moonlit night. She was in bed when she heard the sirens sound, followed by an explosion. The church was a white building standing in its own grounds, and the moonlight possibly 'made it more visible from the air'. Her own house was shaken by the blast, the windows shattered, and slates came off the roof. Although her own family were all safe, a friend of hers lost a father who was fire-watching in the crypt of the church. 'The local men who were in the Home Guard,' she explains, 'took it in turn to be on duty there.' Her own father's name was on the roster, but luckily he was off duty that night.

Elizabeth Berens (née Birch) was a pupil at Hove County Grammar School and one of her most vivid memories is of watching a hockey match on the school playing fields against Brighton & Hove High School when low-flying aircraft flew overhead, guns blazing.

The match was underway, it was about 4pm and a few of us were watching at our school grounds in Nevill Road when the air-raid siren sounded. At this stage in the war, we were so used to this that we took no notice at first, until we heard gunfire and bombs being dropped. The teachers in charge stopped the match and shouted at us to run back to the school building. We were running as fast as we could when a German plane flew over us – the teachers shouted at us to lie down. The plane dived and opened fire. I remember looking up and I could plainly see the swastikas on the plane and even the face of the pilot in the cockpit. I was very frightened. Luckily noone was hit, although two bullets struck the ground near the goal area between two of the players. It would have been obvious to the pilot that this was a group of school children – defenceless – yet he still attacked us. After he had flown past, we all got on our feet and ran as fast as we could back to the safety of the buildings. Needless to say, the hockey match was abandoned, but we did devour the tea, which had been laid out for us.

At the start of the war Ron Green resided in Norwich with his mother Emily and sisters Joyce and June. His father was called-up into the army, having been a territorial beforehand. His grandmother lived in the next street and was often alone as her other sons were in the RAF or serving with the local Home Guard. The old lady was deaf, so when the air-raid siren sounded it was Ron's task to run to her house and get her down her shelter as quickly as possible and return home

132   *Children search for their books in the ruins of their Coventry school.*

133   *ARP workers clear away the rubble from a bombed school in Plymouth, as the pupils look on.*

straight away. However, he admits he did not return before 'Nanny' had presented him with a threepenny bit. His mother and sisters would be waiting under the stairs. They had an Anderson shelter in the garden about two yards from the house but his mother would only use it if the pots and pans hanging on nails under the stairs began to vibrate badly enough to be dislodged, at which point it was a mad rush to the back door.

During the worst bombing of Norwich, in April 1942, the family was cocooned in their shelter when Ron remembers all their doors and windows being blown out as the house opposite took a direct hit. Looking out of the shelter during the daylight raid, he thought the sycamore tree in their garden was laden with snow and longed to make snowballs when it was safe to do so, but the snow turned out to be plaster and other debris from the next block of houses, which he describes as being 'blasted to smithereens'. After the bombing there was nothing left of Globe Street. All that remained of the bakery was the huge oven. The Sunday School he attended was gone and many people were buried under the rubble. Having heard of the destruction of many shops, this eight-year-old boy thought that if he could make it into the city centre he might be able to find some toys in the debris of Woolworths. 'I had a hell of a job getting to the city centre,' he says. 'Police and ARP wardens telling me I couldn't go this way and that. I finally made it almost to Woolworths but a fireman stopped me, he was covered in grey and black dust. In fact Woolies was just a load of girders and there was nothing left, no toys, nothing anywhere. No colours, just greys and blacks and one very dejected little eight-year-old boy.'

Ron now had to make his way home again through the devastated streets, one of which had been blocked off. He had to climb over a wall aided by a small tree but, dropping down the other side, he fell into the arms of an ARP warden. 'Keep still', he said and Ron immediately saw 'a huge bomb tied up with ropes'. The warden carried him a hundred yards or so to Chapel Field Gardens, where he met an older cousin who carried him to safety 'piggy back style'. Ron remembers that the public shelter had been hit and another bomb had wedged itself in the ceiling of the steps that led inside. 'Legend has it,' claims Ron, 'that there are still people buried in that shelter and I could have been one of them.'

Quite often, Avonmouth near Bristol would be the target of raids, enemy aircraft using the river Avon to navigate. Doreen Govan describes how they would first drop thousands of incendiary bombs that caused an unearthly green magnesium fire. This would be followed by heavy bombs jettisoned into the blazing areas. Searchlights swept the skies and ack-ack guns opened up from emplacements on every bit of high ground around the city, but this relentless bombing stretched the emergency services to the limits and beyond.

> These blazes went on all through the winter and spring and a particularly fierce winter it was. At one time, in January, the water froze in the firemen's pipes and huge icicles hung on smoking ruins. During that first Blitz, one event was to be stamped indelibly on my mind. The all clear had gone after a particularly long, heavy raid. I don't think we'd got much sleep that night. Dad came in from fire-watching and said 'Come and have a look at this – you'll never

134 *The aftermath of a direct hit on a public shelter in an unknown south coast town. Much of the shelter seems to have withstood the blast.*

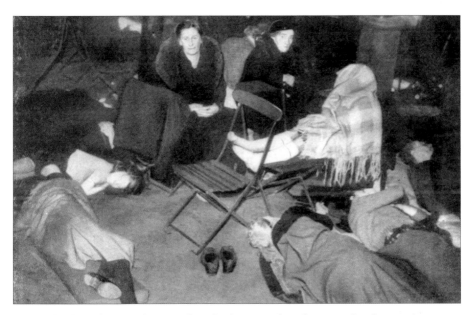

135 *Children sleep as their mothers look on, in this photograph taken in the crypt of a church in Swansea, during one of several heavy attacks.*

believe what you'll see.' I couldn't get out quickly enough but Mum refused to budge and made herself a cup of tea and got back under the stairs. Several of my friends were out in the streets with their dads and we made our way with much excitement to Devon Road Bridge, where the sight that met our eyes was unbelievable. From that vantage point we could see the whole of Down Town and it was ablaze with huge fires as far as the horizon. Whole buildings were going up like torches with a huge pall of smoke overhead. There was still the sound of odd bombs exploding, together with the crash of buildings collapsing. Searchlights still raked the sky. The smell of burning was everywhere. The most memorable sight were the railway lines, all going into the city. In the reflected glow of the fires they looked like scarlet ribbons, some tangled, some straight, but all shining red.

One morning during the Blitz they found an unexploded incendiary bomb had landed in the garden, breaking a bit of trellis. Doreen's mother was furious and stood there in her long green dressing gown and ubiquitous 'Dinkie' curlers firmly crossing her arms over her chest and roundly cursing the intruder. The ARP came and removed the offending article.

Although hardly any district of Bristol was left unscathed, places like Bedminster and Clifton suffering worst being nearest the town centre, for Doreen life went on as before. Each day her route to school might be past the spaces of newly destroyed houses. Piles of rubble would have to be negotiated. Her father worked in the office of a big clothing firm at Temple Meads now making uniforms. The factory was completely destroyed during the first night of the Blitz and was relocated to Twerton near Bath, so for the rest of the war he had to commute there by train. The telephone exchange was also destroyed, so local communication 'was down to walking and finding out for yourself'.

Weston-super-Mare also experienced several nights of intense bombing. Margaret Cable, who was born in 1931, lived in the police house on the Bourneville estate, where her father was the local bobby. A nearby factory manufacturing ammunition was a target for the Germans and the estate was right in the line of fire. One particular night the bombing was extremely heavy.

> My father was on police duty so my mother decided to take both myself and my five-year-old brother down to an air-raid shelter which was in a field at the bottom of our garden. Bombs were exploding and incendiary bombs were hurtling down around us, but I recall I was making a fuss as we sped down the garden path, as I'd lost a shoe and wouldn't be hurried without it. The next day Dad discovered, much to his displeasure, that all the seed potatoes he had recently planted were lying on top of the ground and burnt black! I have never forgotten that night in the air-raid shelter, so dirty, damp and smelly, with just bare concrete walls. There had been no time to take any form of comfort with us, but of course it did the job, we had survived.

After this experience Margaret's parents vowed that during any future raids the family would stay together in one downstairs room. If the worst happened, they would all go together! 'The raiders did not come quite so close the next night,' says Margaret, 'but I do remember Mum finding some pieces of shrapnel on top of the bed. Could they have been there from the night before? We shall never know.'

A few days later, after she was permitted to play outside again, Margaret was bemused to find that many of her normal friends or school mates were nowhere to be seen. 'I was apparently too young to be told there had been direct hits on several houses in the surrounding roads and many of them didn't make the shelter!' Margaret Cable's mother Winifred maintained that during at least one raid the German aeroplanes came so low over the houses of Weston she could see the faces of the pilots. Shortly afterwards, at a time when the city was experiencing its heaviest period of bombing, the children were taken to stay with their grandparents, eight miles from Bristol. Margaret recalls standing in the garden there, watching the sky above the city 'lit up as never before'.

Julie Baker remembers a V2 rocket landing in Gravesend. She was walking back from school when she heard the explosion, and on hurrying home found that a wardrobe had fallen on top of her grandmother. Apart from being a little shaken she was alright. But the next day Julie and her class were informed that one of their school friends had been killed. There was no counselling in those days, she points out. You were just expected to get on with it.

Children in the county of Kent became used to the daily spectacle of dog fights between British and German fighter aircraft during the Battle of Britain, and huge waves of bombers crossing the shoreline. In 1942 Frederick Forsyth was four years old and living in Ashford, brimming with curiosity about the world around him and what he described as the free firework display that took place almost nightly over the heads of those in Kent.

> As darkness fell the drone of the bombers began, heading north west from the Kent coast for London. Others concentrated on the great Ashford railway works a few hundred yards from our house. To my fury I had to spend most of my

136 *Frederick Forsyth remembers the 'free firework display' that took place almost nightly over the heads of those living in Kent.*

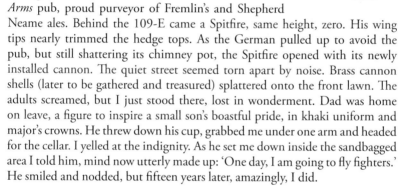

nights and half my days in the cellar. The ack-ack batteries round Ashford would open up in reply; sirens wailed, flashes of shellfire lit up the skies and the search light beams ranged through the blackness, accusing fingers looking for a Heinkel, Junkers or Dornier. By day I stared in wonder at the white contrails high above where Spitfire and Hurricane lunged and parried against Messerschmitt and Focke-Wulf. Then one day at breakfast there was a roar to end all roars. Between the trees at garden-hedge height a Messerschmitt 109-E (one knew them all by sight of course) screamed down Elwick Road right past the breakfast room windows. I could see the German pilot hunched at the controls, the black crosses against the dappled fuselage. At the end of Elwick Road stood the *Kent Arms* pub, proud purveyor of Fremlin's and Shepherd Neame ales. Behind the 109-E came a Spitfire, same height, zero. His wing tips nearly trimmed the hedge tops. As the German pulled up to avoid the pub, but still shattering its chimney pot, the Spitfire opened with its newly installed cannon. The quiet street seemed torn apart by noise. Brass cannon shells (later to be gathered and treasured) splattered onto the front lawn. The adults screamed, but I just stood there, lost in wonderment. Dad was home on leave, a figure to inspire a small son's boastful pride, in khaki uniform and major's crowns. He threw down his cup, grabbed me under one arm and headed for the cellar. I yelled at the indignity. As he set me down inside the sandbagged area I told him, mind now utterly made up: 'One day, I am going to fly fighters.' He smiled and nodded, but fifteen years later, amazingly, I did.

Another city that was severely targetted by the Germans was Southampton, where Pamela Moyse lived as a child in the Woolston area, relatively close to two important factories. One of these was Supermarine, which was concerned with the manufacture of Spitfires, while the other was Thorneycroft, the shipbuilding firm. Pamela lived between the two and recalls that, for a six-year-old girl, it was a living nightmare. In terms of sleep patterns there was no routine and no sense of normality. Night after night they were driven into the Anderson shelter. In the beginning her mother tried to get her to sleep indoors, first under the table and then under the stairs, but as the bombing began in earnest they were forced into their garden refuge. Putting on nightclothes and attempting to go to bed at a regular time became futile, as the sirens would inevitably wail. The shelter she recalls was 'cold, damp and smelly'. Her mother would furnish it with blankets, cushions and pillows, in a bid to make it comfortable, and they would take a wireless and coffee or tea if these were available. For a period they lived here all night, every night. In the early days they would optimistically return to the house when the all clear sounded, but

Pamela describes how, on many occasions the siren would go again just as they got inside. The only time she remembers taking her clothes off was to have a bath, after which she would put clean clothes on, never night garments.

School was not much better. There was a huge shelter but it was not underground, just a reinforced extension to the classroom and the Germans often attacked Southampton in daylight as well as under the cover of night. She likens living around Southampton in September 1940 to being in 'hell'. After one attack on the factories she returned home to discover bodies and body parts strewn around the back garden. The German aircraft were flying overhead and were so low she recalls seeing the faces of the aircrew, both the raiders and the pursuing British pilots. Her father was exempt from the forces as he suffered from flat feet, so he drove a huge petroleum lorry delivering fuel to army bases around the country. On one journey Pamela was accompanying him when a German aircraft came straight towards them. In fear of what might happen if the petrol lorry were hit, her father stopped and the two of them ran for cover. The German raider had been shot and crashed nearby and Pamela describes how her father ran to the aid of the German pilot but the aircraft exploded before he could get anywhere near it. Finally, putting a few essential items on the back of a lorry, they left for the country. 'Southampton was burning everywhere,' remembers Pamela, 'all you could see was a red glow. We managed to find accommodation but had to sleep on the floor as the house was full. Everyone was going to the country to get away from the bombs. My Dad left us there and went back to Southampton to continue his war work, as he put it.'

When Sylvia Cowcill's father was sent overseas, his family moved to Whiston, just outside of Liverpool, to be near her grandparents. Her favourite memories from the time are of being taken into the city by her grandmother. They would visit Lewis's for 'coffee with cream on top', before going down to the docks to watch the ships plying their way along the Mersey or the ferry-boats crossing to New Brighton. The house at which they stayed had a window half way down the stairs, and on one night that Liverpool was heavily bombed Sylvia remembers looking out of it as she was making her way down to the shelter. Outside she could see the searchlights scouring the heavens as bombs exploded in the distance and she was terrified.

At her grandmother's nearby house the family chose to stay in the lounge in preference to the shelter. Her grandmother, step-granddad, aunties and uncles all sat against the walls. That night a bomb fell straight down the middle of the lounge but failed to go off, leaving the luckiest family in Liverpool sitting petrified around the 'dud'. Her grandmother was allowed to keep the nose-cone, which she displayed on the mantelpiece to remind them just how lucky they had been. The next time they went into Liverpool, they discovered that Lewis's had been destroyed. 'I wasn't old enough to realise the scale of the disaster,' she says, 'many people having been killed. I just burst into tears, because there wouldn't be any coffee and cakes in the café.'

At the beginning of the war Maureen Goffin moved with her parents from Hayes in Middlesex to Wallasey in Liverpool, first to stay with an aunt and then in rented accommodation. Her father was a Liverpudlian, the youngest of 15 children. Her parents thought they would be safer in the north than around

London. Wallasey itself received little enemy attention, but she remembers the aftermath of a heavy bombing raid on Liverpool, when the water supply to an area in which her aunts lived was cut off. Her parents decided to help, and filled bottles with water, enough for two large suitcases which they could just manage to carry. They set off by bus and ferry to deliver them, only to find that the trams were not running from the Pier Head. They were forced into emptying the bottles and returning home. Many thousands of people in towns and cities around the country often found themselves without water or power supplies, but in those days there was no water or electricity in more homes anyway, so the disruption would not have been as severe as it would be today.

Housing a busy naval base, Portsmouth was another heavily bombed area. It was home to Tony King, who was five when the war began, and he gives us a vivid insight into what took place in the city. 'My childhood is one long memory of endless nights huddled in a cold Anderson air-raid shelter as the Luftwaffe rained down bombs in an effort to obliterate the huge naval dockyard and railway sidings at Fratton,' he explains. 'The Blitz was just a way of life, and luckily I was young enough not to be really frightened by all the danger and destruction, but old enough to remember much of the chaos that arose as an inevitable consequence.' Every morning Tony would make his way to school, trudging through the rubble-strewn

137   *A grandmother from Liverpool with the four grandchildren, she helped to rescue from their shattered home.*

streets of Portsmouth, looking at smoking ruins yet curiously detached from what he was seeing. Many of his friends had been evacuated, but his mother refused to countenance losing her children, so they spent the entire conflict within the danger zone.

He recalls one particularly cold January night, as he crouched in the shelter and watched the beads of condensation running down the cold metal walls. Outside he could hear the sound of anti-aircraft fire as the city barrage attempted to deter the raiders. Some of the guns were mobile and were moved around the city. On the night in question one was positioned right outside their house. 'Each time it fired,' he says, 'another pane of glass would shatter, and more soot would cascade down the chimney. In the cold light of dawn, it looked as if our home had been bombed.' At the conclusion of that night's aerial activity, Tony went upstairs to his bedroom as usual and remembers peering around the black-out curtains:

> I saw flames flickering against the night as the city blazed in the aftermath of the nightly air raid, throwing a sinister crimson glow across the lowering sky. I could hear the strident bells of the emergency services as they raced through the rubble-strewn streets in their desperate fight to contain the fires and rescue the many poor people trapped in the blazing ruins. I learned many years later, it had been the most serious raid of the war on Portsmouth. Many fine buildings had succumbed that night, along with whole roads of houses close to the dock-yard. The fine guildhall was ablaze, and closer to home I saw the dreadful sight of the hospital burning fiercely. I heard the hoarse shouts of those who were involved in the life or death struggles. In the morning everything carried on as usual. Never was British stoicism better illustrated than in the aftermath of these terrible raids.

Tony describes Portsmouth during the black-out as a 'ghost town'. He remembers the local ARP warden striding up and down the road and bellowing

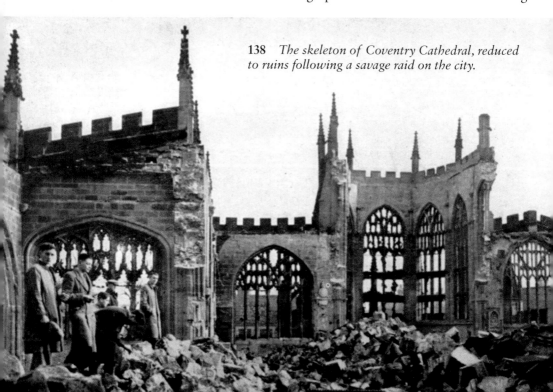

138   *The skeleton of Coventry Cathedral, reduced to ruins following a savage raid on the city.*

139 *A Southampton street after heavy raids on 30 November and 1 December 1940. People return to their ruined homes to salvage a few possessions.*

like a frustrated sergeant major those long-remembered words 'Turn that bloody light off,' if he thought anyone was infringing the regulations. The streets were deserted and enveloped in complete darkness. The few vehicles that ventured out had their headlights covered with hoods. Dark shadows hung over everything, 'waiting expectantly for the ritual sounding of the air-raid siren heralding the opening of yet another night of destruction'.

Was Nowhere Safe?

Bombs were dropped in the most unlikely places, and even in the most remote rural corners children were in danger if a light had been left on and a German aeroplane had bombs left over from its mission. Britain is a relatively small island and most places are not very far from a major urban centre, so many people found themselves under a flight path used by the Germans.

Even in mid-Somerset, Marie Litchfield recalls how the sirens would regularly wail around seven or eight in the evening, announcing to the village that enemy planes would soon be passing over their homes:

> For us, in the depths of the countryside, there was always the presumption that they would be passing over – though we well knew that they might jettison their load of high-explosive bombs anywhere if attacked, before heading for home. Our hearts ached as we thought of the people in the cities they were actually making for. But we had our little procedure, at any rate at the beginning of the war. As it went on, everyone became more used to it, and

140 *Len, the brother of Iris Thomas, was in the Air Training Corps before joining the RAF. During air raids he would put an enamel washing-up bowl on his head and watch the action from the garden.*

took fewer precautions. If we had already gone to bed when the siren sounded, we would get up, pick up our 'air raid bundles' and go downstairs in our dressing-gowns to the living-room. These bundles were something people were encouraged to make – a little collection of things they might need when in an air-raid shelter, so that they didn't suddenly decide to rush back and get some vital requisite. I always took my knitting-bag in my bundle, having heard that knitting was recommended as soothing to the nerves!

At Boddington, where the father of Iris Thomas worked at a rural manor, children soon realised they were unlikely targets for German bombers. There were two anti-aircraft batteries nearby, and if the sirens sounded the kids would go out to watch the searchlights switch on and the guns open up. They would enjoy the spectacle with little thought of danger, and without rushing into any shelters. However, things could have been very different. Boddington itself was rural and of no interest to the enemy, but its position close to Staverton Airfield placed it in a danger zone.

Iris' brother Len, who was in the Air Training Corps and later joined the RAF, would rush outside to try and spot any aircraft. Iris remembers his mother shouting at him not to be a silly idiot and come inside. His response was to put an enamel washing-up bowl on his head before heading back out to continue his vigil. 'After the raids,' says Iris, 'we would all collect odd bits of shrapnel which had fallen nearby.' On one clear night during one such raid, no doubt aimed at Gloucester, Len and his father were in the garden when they saw something falling towards the house. Iris' father shouted a warning and they all rushed towards the cupboard under the stairs. Luckily the bomb landed in a big garden about a mile and a half away without hurting anyone. The second bomb to land around Boddington, fell near the school, fortunately at night when it was empty of children.

When my mother took me to school the following morning she told me we would visit the bomb site on the way. I really looked forward to seeing this and had a vision of a lovely neat hole in the brown soil surrounded by untouched grass. I was so disappointed with the reality. I can still picture the sight today, an untidy, ugly mess of clay and stones, thrown all over the place, and several shocked-looking villagers standing around peering into the hole.

There were two more bombs in the area, both of which fell about a quarter of a mile from their cottage, behind the church. Despite landing in a field containing cows, none was hurt as they were all congregating near the farm waiting to be milked.

Marie Litchfield also writes about the odd occasions when her village of Ashcott was bombed.

> There was a very frightening day when a bomber raid took place in broad daylight. We were all in the stone-flagged courtyard at the back of the house looking up into the blue sky, watching the bombers flying over, high up but clearly visible. Then suddenly there was the terrible whine of a falling high-explosive bomb. We ran frantically indoors, but then … nothing. Silence. For a long time we felt the explosion must come. But it didn't. Apparently the bomb had fallen in a field near the High Street but had not gone off. Experts came and rendered it safe, but it made us realise that we were vulnerable, despite our distance from any large town. On another occasion, two oil-bombs fell in an orchard close by our house. These did go off, but because there was nothing nearby to ignite the oil, no fire ensued. The trees, hedges and lane were bespattered with oil, and bits of twisted metal from the bombs were scattered over a wide area. Children collected them as souvenirs – Ashcott's bombs – and played with them.

Although June Richards lived at Axmouth along the south Devon coast, and away from any real danger zones, she recalls getting into trouble with her father several times, because of enemy aircraft. As she was coming home from Sunday School two aeroplanes were fighting, so she climbed an apple tree to get a closer look. The next minute her father was pulling her down in order to take her home to the shelter. Then machine guns started to fire and he pushed her into a ditch with muddy water in it. 'My best Sunday dress was in an awful state,' she recalls. The cream floral dress had apparently been made from a panel taken from the lounge curtains. On another occasion, she remembers being in the playground and watching a very low flying aircraft with big black crosses on the wings. She

141 *Was nowhere safe? Even here at Bridge of Waith in the Orkney Islands a cottage is bombed out. This picture emphasises the fact that every corner of Britain was not that far away from a military presence. In this instance the bombers were attracted by the naval anchorage at Scapa Flow.*

ran to tell the teacher, who did not believe her. But when she got home it was a very different story as her father had seen the plane himself. She was 'tapped on the wrist' with a ruler, because she should not have stood and watched it.

Although she lived on a farm near Glentham in Lincolnshire, Mary Cooper often felt in the thick of it as they were near the RAF stations at Scampton and Hemswell. A lot of bombs were dropped around them, one of which fell in April but wasn't found until harvest time because it ended up in the middle of a cornfield and was only discovered when Mary's uncle began harvesting. The bomb squad closed all the roads and detonated it, after which shrapnel was found up to two miles away. Incendiary bombs were dropped which resulted in burning hedges. One night several bombs were dropped near the farm one landing just down the road in the ditch, others in a wood just below the house. These were never found as far as Mary is aware and she wonders if they are still there to this day?

Margaret Wilce recalls the bombs that fell around the small village of Walford near Ross-on-Wye, where her father was an ARP warden. On one occasion a stick of bombs was dropped along the riverbank at Bishopswood, and bombs dropped on Leys Hill resulted in minor damage and broken windows at a cottage whose elderly residents her father had to rescue. Margaret's father was quite certain the area was targetted because of the poor intelligence of the enemy. During the First World War there had been a munitions factory at Lydbrook (Edison Swan Cables) and he was confident this was their target, even though it was no longer concerned with the manufacture of munitions.

One night, as the sirens sounded, her father went into the garden and observed an aircraft caught in the beam from the searchlight on Coppett Hill. An airman was seen to bail out and the light followed him all the way down to some trees at Oxlet Woods near Bishopswood. Her father was among the wardens and other services that tried unsuccessfully to find him, much to her mother's disappointment as she could have made good use of the parachute silk. He turned out to be British. In the dark he had found his way out of the woods and arrived at a farmhouse, where Daphne Jones, the young girl who lived there with her father, without knowing for sure if he were British, guided him along a narrow footpath to the home of Major Gaskill-Davies. His was the nearest house with a telephone and the pilot was able to report to his squadron that he was safe. His aircraft was later recovered from the River Wye at Lydbrook.

At Whitchurch in Shropshire, Joyce Copper also recalls the sight of descending parachutes. 'We often had to shelter under the stairs,' she says, 'when bombers flew over to drop their load on Liverpool or Manchester, and although we were 47 miles away we could see the red glow in the sky after these raids. Just occasionally one of these planes jettisoned a left-over bomb near us on its return journey but they didn't cause a great deal of damage.' One day, when she was riding her bike with some friends, they saw a German aircraft being shot down, and the crew descending on their parachutes. 'We were filled with childish fury,' she explains, 'and threatened to do terrible things to them if we found them, so cycled in their direction. Of course we would not have been able to carry out our threats even if we had actually discovered one of these airmen. Anyway, we were stopped by the police who were blocking the road and sent home.'

Chapter 9

From Agony to Ecstasy

Children were not only in danger from direct bombing, but also from dangerous ordnance that littered the countryside. Because Britain remained an island fortress for six years even friendly ordnance could cause a danger if left unattended. Dangers lurked around many corners, especially given the fact that children, by their very nature, are inquisitive. But as Hitler attempted to postpone his inevitable downfall with the use of V weapons, the war had already entered its final, bloody, phase. Soon the children of Britain would be lifted out of their agony, into a victory that for many came at a terrible price.

Danger on the Doorstep

June Richards at Axmouth recalled the people at her end of the village being told to leave their homes and proceed to the other end and congregate in the schoolroom. This was because her brother, who had earlier been sent up the road to fetch milk, had discovered a parachute in a field attached to a 'device' stuck in the ground, reported it to his family, and received a tap on the wrist for admitting he had touched it. June's eldest brother was sent to fetch Mr Abbott, the local special constable, who in turn alerted Police Sergeant Abrahams in Seaton, the nearest town.

The two officers investigated the object as the villagers looked on. They told the crowd to move further down the village and wait for the arrival of an army bomb disposal team. The army team didn't know how to deal with the object and sent for their opposite numbers in the RAF. They could do nothing either and the Royal Navy was summoned, who knew exactly what it was and what to do. June explains that the object proved to be a Royal Navy torpedo jettisoned from an aircraft before it crashed. 'As the crow flies it was only half a mile to the sea,' explains June. The pilot, finding himself in trouble, must have assumed the torpedo would land in the water. It took two days to disarm and dig it out of the ground, during which time the villagers had to camp out in the schoolroom. The object was 22 feet long and June recalls that when it was finally driven away it hung for some distance over the back of the lorry.

At St Margaret's at Cliffe, the young Frank Stanford knew a local farmer called Mr Wier who ran Solton Manor Farm at nearby East Langdon. Frank's father was the village blacksmith so he would often shoe Mr Wier's horses, or repair his farm machinery. Frank, who was 12 became very friendly with Mr Wier's daughter Jean, but sadly his father closed the forge, sold up and took his family to the Tonbridge area, so Frank and Jean were forced to say goodbye. 'The bombing and shelling drove many of us from the Kent coast,' explains Frank. He did not

142   *On 24 August 1940 a Messerschmitt Bf 109E crash landed on Solton Manor Farm in Kent. Jean Wier, the daughter of the farmer is sitting in the cockpit, surrounded by British soldiers. The pilot, Fritz Beeck, who had been shot down by a Hurricane of 56 Squadron RAF, gave himself up.*

hear from Jean again until 2004 when he discovered she was living in Scotland. He knew that not long after he left a Messerschmitt Bf 109E had been forced down on Mr Wier's land and often wondered whether Jean had been there at the time. So imagine his surprise when all those years later she sent him a photograph, taken by her mother, of herself sitting in the cockpit of the German fighter being guarded by British soldiers.

One of Frank's childhood pleasures in early 1940, was visiting St Margaret's Bay before it was fortified with metal, barbed wire and concrete to stop enemy troops landing on the beach. On one such visit he discovered a bomb, about four feet long and painted yellow, lying under two feet of water. He and his friends rather recklessly tried to remove it from the water as the tide was out but it proved far too heavy for them, so they sent for more help. There were two ways to visit St Margaret's Bay, down either a steep winding road or hundreds of wooden steps. The gang of 11- and 12-year-olds, having eventually removed the bomb from the water, decided to take it up the steps. The task took hours but that did not matter to Frank: 'This was my bomb and I was taking it home as a souvenir.' At the top of the hill, two of the lads were sent to bring back a four-wheel truck that somebody had. 'It was still a mile to go before reaching my home,' he continues. On the way the hapless group were stopped by an army officer, who asked where they had discovered their cargo. He agreed to let them keep their souvenir, and confirmed that as it had been found under water it was perfectly safe. A little further on they were stopped by the village policeman and, after being told that an army officer had given them the OK, he also allowed them to continue.

'So it stood against my downstairs bedroom window for two weeks,' says Frank. During that time, he and his friends often pushed it around on the four-wheel truck, and several service people stopped to admire it. However, when his brother Arthur who was in the Royal Navy arrived home on leave from his base at Chatham it was quite a different story. 'As he got near the house,' recalls Frank, 'he dropped his kit bag and ran to a telephone box.' He then made every one move away from the houses and out of the nearby post office. Just over one hour later the Royal Navy mine and bomb disposal team arrived from Chatham Dockyard. They took the bomb down to the bay with a crowd following at a safe distance, and proceeded to explode it. 'I got a good telling off by the naval officer in charge,' continues Frank, 'in spite of me telling him an army officer had seen the bomb and allowed me to have it. He said it was a German delayed action bomb and could have exploded at any time, even though it was found under water. Just by chance my brother Arthur had attended a lecture about these bombs a week before coming home on leave.'

Joy Matthews who lived in the small town of Eye in Suffolk has a rather happier memory of unexploded bombs. Their house was on the flight path of both allied and German planes, as was most of East Anglia. Joy was playing in the front garden when she saw an enemy plane drop a stick of bombs over the town, about a mile away. She informed her mother, who hauled her up to the police station to describe what she had seen. Later that day there was a knock on the door and a soldier stood on the front doorstep: 'We have got something to show the little girl, will you bring her to the front gate.'

'Coming up the road,' smiles Joy, 'were some khaki clad figures pushing a wheelbarrow. In the barrow were some bombs with a soldier sitting astride one. They were shouting and waving for us to come and have a look. The bombs had fallen in the yard of a local outfitters and not exploded. The bomb disposal boys had defused them and they were being taken for safe keeping to the police station, but first they wanted to take them to show the little girl. What an exciting afternoon.'

143   *This picture taken on the Yorkshire coast shows members of a Royal Navy bomb disposal team making safe a German mine, which had been washed up on the shore.*

144   *'Hundred Proof' by Joe Crowfoot. Two boys and their dog playing in the East Anglian countryside watch the familiar sight of a B-17 Flying Fortress of the 100th Bomb Group fly overhead.*

Many people had close encounters with various types of explosive device. Jean Pearse used to go walking on Mothecombe beach near her Devon home, until it was mined and placed out of bounds, but this did not stop local people venturing along the coast. Two individuals, thinking they could walk between the mines, were blown up and killed and no children went on the beach after that. Colin Webb had a close encounter with a mine on Brighton seafront while coming home from school. Colin and a couple of mates watched as a soldier was clearing mines from the beach.

> He was driving a tank and using a strong jet of water to bring mines to the surface. He climbed out and was walking towards us when there was a loud explosion. His remains landed in barbed wire about a foot away from where we were standing. I was thirteen years old at the time and had many nightmares.

Johnny Ringwood had a lucky escape while playing on a bomb site in the Custom House area of London. Children seemed to be drawn to places of danger and Johnny describes bomb sites as being like 'adventure playgrounds'. One day his two mates, Jimmy and Davie Lee, were not so lucky and 'copped it' while playing among the ruins. Johnny had just left them because his mother wanted some errands run. He was going through the front door, when there was an almighty blast caused by a V2 rocket landing on the site where the boys were playing, killing them and another boy called Sparrow.

Aircraft would also fall to earth from time to time. These could be German or allied, but either way they would attract the attentions of local children hungry for souvenirs. Frank Hind recalls a Messerschmitt Bf 110 fighter bomber crash landing in a field about half a mile from his home. His plans to retrieve gunpowder and ammunition from the crash site were thwarted by the police, who kept small boys well away from the scene. At Boddington, Iris Thomas remembers a Hotspur glider coming down behind some trees when she was on her way home from school on 4 September 1942. It had been trying to land at No. 3 Glider Training School at nearby RAF Stoke Orchard. She and her friends rushed over to investigate but were stopped by the farmer, who told them not to enter the field. It was just as well, because when the emergency services arrived the first thing they did was remove the body, of a certain Corporal Palmer. Later, the children were permitted into the field to examine the remains of the aircraft and collect small pieces of the fuselage.

The sight of dead and mutilated bodies was one of the many horrors that children in Britain often came face to face with. They witnessed terrible scenes of brutality that disturbed them. At Avoch, one of the most distressing things that Donald Patience witnessed was a group of soldiers who tied up a dog and shot it. He does not know why this was done, but he felt terrible for a long time afterwards.

145 *The black cross and swastika on a Dornier DO17 shot down by the RAF. Children would flock to crash sites to collect souvenirs, but were normally held back by the security services.*

One of Jean Bradley's most unpleasant wartime memories involves her own pet dog. She lived in Coventry and her new puppy was just a few months old when her mother asked her to go to the shop across the road, a busy thoroughfare leading towards Leicester. She left the front door ajar, went down the path and, pulled the gate shut behind her – or so she thought. The road was busy with army vehicles and on the way back she had to wait some time to cross as a convoy of American lorries was passing. Across the road she could see her mother waiting by the gate, looking forlorn. Apparently Sandy, the puppy, had been run over as he tried to follow Jean across the road. She remembers asking her mother, 'He will be alright in a minute, won't he?' It was a few days before Christmas.

When June Richards walked down to the waterside one day, about a quarter of a mile from her home, she found a number of her friends arguing as to whether a horse or a pig had been washed up on one of the islands in the River Axe. She waded out to see for herself, only to discover the body was that of an airman. 'I remember to this day,' she says, 'a hand with little flesh on it, but a big gold ring still on the finger. I rushed back to the road and told my friends it was a pig and then ran up to the house of our special constable, Mr Abbott, who looked for himself before alerting the appropriate services. We all stood and watched the body being removed.'

There was a tendency to exaggerate, or play tricks. In Portsmouth, Tony King recalls one of his friends coming to school clutching a large bone. He solemnly assured them this was all that remained of 'Mrs 'iggins' who lived in the house opposite his own until it had been 'blitzed'. 'Ghoulish ignoramuses that we were,' says Tony, 'we believed him, and it wasn't until some time later that I suspected that what he had actually discovered was an old bone given to a dog!'

Philip Everest, who was evacuated to Crowborough in Sussex to escape the dangers faced by children in London, relates an extremely sad tale. On 8 November 1940 he was playing with a friend, a local boy who was only four and a half years old. Philip himself was two weeks short of his seventh birthday. They were walking along the road together when two aircraft suddenly appeared overhead, one pursuing the other and firing its guns. 'Suddenly' Philip recalls, 'my friend dropped to the ground with a hole in the side of his neck. He died of his injuries on 12 December 1940 at the Kent and Sussex Hospital. On the day of his funeral I saw him in his coffin; he was so small. He was an only child and the parents were devastated.' Philip has always felt that, being the older of the two, he was somehow responsible for the little boy's death.

Colin Webb was 12 years old when his father was invalided out of the Royal Navy and purchased 49 Regency Square, Brighton, in 1942. A large brick-built water tank about six feet deep was placed on the green in the middle of the square, where there were also slit trenches and an ammunition dump. The *Beach Hotel* was empty, and occasionally used by the ARP, and a few other local hotels on the eastern side of the square were occupied by Polish airmen. The whole area became something of a playground for the local children, who would sneak into the basement of the *Beach Hotel* and ride up and down in the dumb waiter. In 1944 the fire brigade emptied the water tank, so local kids climbed inside to see what they could find on its bottom. They discovered a few pennies and several rounds of ammunition and took the bullets to one of the slit trenches and built a fire, into which the bullets were lobbed. They heard them explode but could not see them, so somebody fetched the lid of a pig swill bin and laid it on top of the fire. The bullets were dropped on top of this, and when they exploded the boys could watch them from the lip of the trench. The bullets made quite a sharp noise, but surprisingly nobody came to investigate. Next they discovered 'this whopper of a shell' which they also put on the fire. 'We knew that this one would make a big bang,' states Colin, 'so we hid in the air-raid shelters that were built in the road outside the houses. When it did go off, it broke several windows.' This time, within minutes, the emergency services including the police, fire brigade and army arrived to investigate the explosion. They were far too busy to ask Colin and his small gang if they knew anything, so the boys decided to wander home without volunteering any intelligence.

The Beginning of the End

In the early months of 1944, the island fortress prepared for what would arguably be the most important single battle of the 20th century, the D-Day landings of 6 June, a day that would herald the start of the closing phase of the Second World War. The armies of many nations funnelled towards the south of England, turning numerous counties into huge military transit camps. For a short period it seemed that soldiers were everywhere and children were excited by their presence.

In late May 1944 Doreen Govan was in her final year at grammar school. One day the whole class was distracted by the sound of vehicles in the main road outside and when break eventually came they dashed out to satisfy their curiosity.

146 *In the early months of 1944, huge areas of Britain were turned into military transit camps. Here a convoy of howitzers moves through a quiet English village.*

The girls' playground included a walled platform outside the main door, which was soon crammed with pupils. They observed what seemed to be an endless stream of army vehicles going along the road. There were trucks, lorries, half-tracks and guns mounted on carriers, every conceivable piece of machinery and, of course, every vehicle had its full complement of soldiers. 'I think the appreciation was reciprocal,' notes Doreen, 'as the strong bevy of teenaged girls waved and shouted and blew kisses to the soldiers who responded enthusiastically with cheers and wolf whistles. Rather surprisingly no prefect or teacher was sent to restrain our enthusiasm.'

The county of Dorset was particularly busy and Gerald Bartlett lived in Portesham, an area largely taken over by the Americans. His grandfather was the local butcher and every Tuesday he would drive his van to Weymouth to collect a block of ice, the only way of keeping raw meat cool before there were refrigerators. On the Tuesday before the invasion Gerald and his mother observed a very long convoy of DUKWs heading towards Weymouth. 'My mother was worried that her father would be travelling back in the opposite direction,' he recalls. 'So we set out on foot from Portesham and walked on the grass verge until we eventually met him. He had managed to park in the gateway to a field and here we waited with him until the convoy had passed. I am sure he was greatly relieved.'

Anne Biffin's house at Testwood was on the A36, the route between Salisbury and Southampton. Her father, being a builder and in a reserved occupation, was involved with the construction of the Mulberry Harbour. Before D-Day there were endless convoys of troops passing their gate and when the lorries stopped for a rest the soldiers would sit along the ditches outside the houses, where Anne and her mother would take them jugs of tea. They had no idea these men were part of an invasion force.

147 *British soldiers on the march somewhere in southern England, training for the forthcoming campaign in Europe.*

148   *In this photograph, probably taken on a beach in East Anglia, men of the Suffolk Regiment storm on to the sand dunes.*

Throughout Monday 5 June, lines of ships and landing craft moved out of ports along the south coast of England to form the greatest armada ever assembled. The British and Canadians would attack the beaches code-named Gold, Juno and Sword, at the eastern side of the invasion front, so they embarked from ports along the south-east coast of England, from Harwich and the Thames Estuary to Portsmouth and Southampton. The Americans would attack Omaha and Utah beaches, so they embarked from ports in the south-west of the country. Although many Americans sailed from Southampton, the main force set out from between Falmouth in the west and Poole in the east, and took in the ports of Plymouth, Salcombe, Dartmouth, Brixham, Torbay, Portland and Weymouth.

At Hove, Elizabeth Berens can recall watching the armada of ships as it made its way to France. That evening she was supposed to attend a youth club meeting, but it was cancelled and a church service was held instead in St Peter's Church, West Blatchington, to pray for the troops taking part in the invasion. At Faversham in Kent, Allan George recalls how the 'sky was full of aircraft towing gliders on their trip across the Channel to France'.

Portsmouth, the home of Bill Hawkins, was of particular importance throughout the build-up to the invasion. Bill recalls that from 1943 'the tide of war began to change, from defensive to offensive'. The entire sea front, from Eastney to Portsmouth Harbour, had been a militarised zone for many years, and members of the public were kept at bay by thick rows of barbed wire, and guarded entry and egress points, but with the country's changing fortunes this became a vast training area for the D-Day landings.

Despite all the security, Bill and his friend Geoff had ways of getting into the zone. The most effective one was to emulate the tactics of real commandos observed on Pathe News reels. They would crawl beneath the wire and through Lumps Fort to a concealed observation post in a small dip in the ground between bushes. From here they had a panoramic view of the Solent and the beach from Eastney Point to South Parade Pier:

> The naval anchorage of Spithead appeared to be jammed full of ships of all shapes and sizes. We watched in amazement as funny looking boats with flat fronts ran onto the shore disgorging dozens of heavily armed soldiers who would charge up the pebbled beach and stop at the roadside. Meanwhile, other soldiers would be boarding similar craft from several piers that jutted out into the sea. These piers, made only from lengths of scaffolding bars with a wooden planked walkway on top, seemed very flimsy to carry so many men. Wherever we looked we saw chaos – or so it seemed. There were lorries and marching troops on the road, and tanks and troops running up and down the stone beach. The tanks were running on what looked like rubber matting. All this was accompanied by the deafening roar of explosions that caused the sea to shoot up in the air and then, after a short pause, cascade back down again in a downpour of solid water. And there were dozens of uniformed men running around shouting, blowing whistles and waving flags like demented train guards. Sat where I was, I would not have liked to be a German defender facing them.

149 *Victory party in Belson Road, Woolwich. Margaret Thipthorpe is sitting second row up on far left in light dress and pigtails.*

Occasionally, Bill and Geoff's attention was attracted by small numbers of men from Eastney Royal Marine Barracks dressed in black rubber-suits and flippers, who disappeared into the water, while others dressed in similar fashion would paddle furiously around in two-man canoes. Bill did not realise that he was watching the elite Special Boat Service (SBS) in training, nor that in later life he himself would do identical things on the same stretch of beach. With a father who was a Royal Marine, perhaps that was inevitable.

Following D-Day, Bill explains that these landing craft and other ships brought back the thousands of wounded troops from France. 'These poor souls were put ashore at Portsmouth Dockyard into a massive fleet of ambulances to be transported the short distance across the city to Fratton Railway Station, where they parked, two deep, on both sides of Goldsmith Avenue, which had been closed to public traffic for all of its two-mile length. Here they queued, waiting for the hospital trains that would take them to hospitals all over the country.'

150 *Mothers and babies enjoy the victory celebrations in Pastor Street in the Elephant and Castle area of London.*

As a new member of the Sea Cadet Corps, Bill willingly volunteered to assist the Women's Voluntary Service who were working in Goldsmith Avenue at the time. The women piled boxes of 'goodies' into the arms of helpers, to be passed on to the poor men in the ambulances, while they drove green canteen vans up and down the Avenue handing out cups of tea and buns. The 'goodies' that Bill and the other Sea Cadets handed out included bottled water, biscuits, notepaper and pencils, cigarettes and toilet paper. Their job was to pass a box to each ambulance driver for him to distribute among his passengers. However, most drivers were in the back of the parked vehicles giving what comfort they could to the wounded. Consequently, the young helpers came into close contact with a great many of the suffering troops, swathed in blooded bandages and crippled by terrible injuries. 'What I never saw or heard,' he concludes, 'was any moaning or groaning from the troops who were obviously suffering from a lot of pain. Mostly, they were laughing and joking and taking the mickey out of us young boys by saying things like, "When did you get back from the other side, mate?" Being called "mate" by these soldiers who had been through hell made us feel like men.'

Victory in Europe

On 8 May 1945 the war in Europe finally came to an end. VE Day was marked around the nation by street parties and other events. It is always claimed that the end of the Japanese war on 2 September 1945 was a much less celebrated affair, and the accounts in this book of people's wartime lives explain why. From 3 September 1939, until the total collapse of Nazi Germany, this had been a people's war, a children's war, everybody in Britain being involved and everybody sharing the danger. The campaign in the Far East was more like the colonial wars of preceding centuries: it was a soldier's war fought in a distant land, although children would still be affected by the conflict with Japan, as fathers and other male family members were absent from home. For the people of Britain the dangers had ceased and, although it would take some time to recover, children could begin to get back to normality. Many youngsters had known nothing but war during their entire lives.

'At last came the news we had waited six long years for,' says Doreen Govan, 'the war in Europe was over. VE Day! Hitler was dead, Berlin had fallen. Everyone went wild. I don't remember much work or schooling going on, but I suppose it must have done. People were thronging all the main streets of the towns. On the

151   *A couple of Land Army girls taking the children of Wigston for a ride in a highly decorated cart during victory celebrations.*

152   *VE Day street party in Bruce Avenue, Easton, in Bristol.*

newsreels we saw people in Trafalgar Square climbing on the statues. Down came the hated black-out curtains and on came the lights.' Where all the red, white and blue came from Doreen does not recall, but every house in Bristol had some display in its windows, together with pictures of the King, Queen and Winston Churchill. Streets tried to outdo each other with patriotic decorations. Strings of flags and bunting were draped across roads from window to window. Doreen enjoyed walking around the streets, assessing the best displays.

Then came the street parties and every conceivable scrap of stored food was pooled for the pleasure of all. The baker made buns for every child in the road, with their name iced on the top. Although Doreen was now 16 she still qualified for one of these cakes. Tables were brought out and laid end to end down the middle of the road and all the kids had a sit-down tea. In the evening there was a big bonfire party and someone produced a gramophone to play records on. This was mainly intended for adults, so Doreen put on her favourite dress, made by her mother using material bought with coupons. It was silk, with a sweetheart neckline, puff sleeves and a swinging flared skirt, all in shades of blue and mauve. 'No one had stockings,' she notes, 'and the fashion was to paint our legs with anything from cocoa powder to gravy browning, which was very sticky. I got mine a nice shade of brown, but Dad refused to paint black seams on them.' Food appeared as if by magic and, although there was alcohol for the men, Doreen does not recall any unruliness. Everybody came out and the bonfire was kept alight by adding anything available to burn. A new teacher had moved into the street from Wales, with his wife and daughter and when the music got going he decided he was going to teach Doreen to dance; she admits to finding the experience of going round

153   *VE Day bonfire at Penygraig in Rhondda.*

154 *Celebrations at Hutton School in Essex to mark Victory in Europe.*

and round the bonfire very enjoyable. However, 'Mum was not best pleased,' she confesses, 'as she thought he should have been dancing with his wife, not picking up young girls. Needless to say, I should not have encouraged him either.'

Festivities both organised and impromptu seemed to go on for weeks that summer in Bristol, before things began to settle back down again. The city had to be rebuilt, men returned home, lost ones mourned, and lives restarted.

In Oxford, Miriam Margolyes, who has since appeared in films ranging from *Harry Potter and the Chamber of Secrets* to *Little Shop of Horrors*, has very vivid memories of the victory celebrations among the dreaming spires. Her father was a doctor whose patients had included American personnel at the US army base in Upper Heyford, who she remembers giving the family tins of Del Monte pineapple.

My favourite memory of War was actually of the first day of peace on May 8 1945. My energetic and patriotic mother, who came to Oxford with my father because their house in Plaistow, East Ham, was bombed as they cowered in the cellar below, decided that the best way to mark VE Day was to feed the bus crews, who were still driving buses along the Banbury Road where we lived, even on the Day itself. We started preparing sandwiches and cakes from early morning. I was four but the thrill that day of setting up a stall on the pavement and running out in the middle of the road has never left me. We set up the trestle tables festooned with Union Jacks, right outside our house at 159a Banbury Road. We piled them full of tomato sandwiches sliced thin by Mummy, who was really the champion tomato slicer of all time. There were egg sandwiches, cheese sandwiches, probably beef sausage sandwiches and lots of jam sandwiches, but no pork – we were Jewish and got extra cheese rations instead. The bread was white and I suspect it was margarine and not butter, which was rationed. Every few minutes, my mother ran inside to the kitchen and got more boiling water for the tea. I manned the stall alone, waving all the time – everyone waved back.

Mummy baked lots of little cakes and apple tarts and some cheese cake. Jewish cakes are heavy, very fattening and delicious. The bus crews saw me waving frantically and they stopped and I would run out into the road and my mother lifted me up to the level of the driver's cab, and I'd pass through the cups of heavily sweetened tea (bang goes the sugar ration) and the plates of sandwiches. The crews were tickled pink. It seemed no one else in Oxford had this thought, so we became quite famous. Each time a bus passed, it stopped. One of my father's patients was a gorgeous ex-cockney called Mrs Penny – a fitting name for a bus conductress. She was on the 93 bus to Kidlington. Every 30 minutes or so, Mrs Penny stopped for a cuppa and I'd get on the bus too and be cuddled by the passengers. And Mummy was slicing and spreading and arranging for hours and I helped with the washing up. All day I was eating and being cuddled – such activity has remained my favourite. We were uncompli-catedly happy: now we knew there was an end to the War and all of its horrors. Could anything be more delightful? It really was Peace and Love – so long ago, in those innocent days when I was young.

Margaret Cable remembers that in Weston-super-Mare every household gave a dish of food to help fill the trestle tables which lined their street, Lonsdale Avenue. A clear memory she has is of the number of young girls there who were heavily pregnant! She was simply told this was due to the 'friendly invasion' of the American soldiers.

Also in Somerset, Frank Hind recalls the VE Day bonfire on which children burnt effigies of their recent foes, Hitler and Mussolini. In Devizes Bill Underwood remembers a large bonfire built on Roundway Hill where, in the evening, three of his family walked to join in with the communal singing.

At Flimby in Cumbria, Ethel Fisher recalls the musical entertainment that livened up their huge bonfire on the shores of the Solway Firth, at a place called Long and Small. A local man played the piano and Ethel accompanied him on an accordion that her father had bought her. He had also managed to acquire the sheet music of several wartime hits. 'All the locals joined in the singing,' she proudly claims, 'and a good time was had by all, until well after midnight when the festivities eventually stopped.' By that time all the food had been eaten, the bonfire was reduced to ashes, and the voices were too hoarse to continue. Geoff Grater recalls the scene in Tiverton, when Mrs Lake, who lived opposite him, dragged her piano out into the street to provide music. All the adults had saved up food for the occasion and another feast ensued.

At Broadstone School in Dorset, in order to help them come to terms with peace, the pupils were asked to write a composition describing their understanding of the formal German surrender. Roy Stevens was now ten years old and the following was his effort, complete with errors in punctuation and spelling, for which he received a VG from the teacher!

155   *Among the celebrations in Weston-super-Mare was a beauty contest, won by the fourteen year old Margaret Cable, seen here proudly holding her trophy.*

The Declaration of Peace

It is a famous street in Berlin the building is a dreary house which used to serve as an Engineering College inside are two long tables. on one table are seated the Russian, British, American and French delegates and the other table is emty. At last the german delegates arrive headed by field marshal Kietel. they take their places and the signing is ready to begin. Marshal Zhoukov asks Marshal Kietel if he agree's the answer is 'yes I agree'. In a few minutes the declaration is signed and it is all over. Marshal Zhoukov says the German delagates may leave.

At Whitchurch in Shropshire, Joyce Copper recalls how VE Day was celebrated by a firework display in the town park put on by the American base. It turned out to be an unforgettable event and probably as dangerous as anything experienced during the war. Someone accidentally dropped a cigarette end or cigar butt into the box of fireworks, which proceeded to go off in every direction. 'It was a case of lay flat or suffer the consequences,' she explains. 'We kids thought it was a great laugh but I'm sure our parents were not so happy about it, though it certainly ended our war with a bang. Luckily not a deadly one!'

Homecoming

The war in Europe was finally over and family life soon returned to its pre-war format, although for some children there was still one important missing ingredient, a father figure. Many men would remain in uniform for some time to come, especially those still fighting in the Far East and facing the daunting prospect of invading mainland Japan. However, many of those serving in Europe were immediately released. Where children were concerned this had varying affects, which were not always for the best.

156   *Victory races held at the village of Ancroft in Northumberland shortly after VE Day.*

157   *Geoffrey Burgon and his mother.*

Geoffrey Burgon, whose best known works include the score for 'Brideshead Revisited', was born in 1941. His father joined the army at the outset of the war, on active service with the Royal Artillery almost throughout. He was a complete stranger to his son, who believes his own conception must have occurred during a period of leave his father enjoyed in 1940:

In the meantime I lived with my mother, her parents and her three sisters, in a mill house idyllically situated in a remote part of Hampshire. The nearest village to Mill Court, where I lived, is Binsted, which is between Alton and Farnham. Having had my mother's undivided attention for the best part of four years, it isn't surprising that I didn't share her enthusiasm for my father when he returned in 1945. Who was this stranger who barged in and took her away from me? I remember details of the day vividly. All the adults sitting around the dining table at lunchtime, whilst I sulked on the floor. I can even remember the floral patterned dinner plates that were used.

The next day my father took my mother to the cinema, and I was left at the garden fence as they walked up the long track to the road, screaming to my mother to come back. But it wasn't all bad. One day my father made a raft out of two oil drums and some planks of wood, and sailed it, with me aboard, on the mill pond next to our house. Then he went away again for a few months and in the meantime we moved from idyllic Hampshire to a dull London suburb. My father returned shortly afterwards, and life was quite different. It took years for me to accept him, and discover what a great father he really was.

I was only four years old when the war in Europe ended, and living where we did it hardly impinged on us directly. Though I do remember that years later my mother told me she waited anxiously for the postman every day, expecting the dreaded telegram, and I suspect that her anxiety got through to me, as to this day I feel a certain anticipation every time I see the postman arrive. Her anxiety was completely understandable as my father saw action in many of the most dangerous theatres of the war, including North Africa, Italy, France and Germany. He was also one of the last to be evacuated from Dunkirk. However, he escaped injury until VE Day itself, when he rode his motor bike into a shell hole and broke his arm.

Deanna Allan admits that she used to boast about being a war baby until someone took her aside and explained, 'I wouldn't brag about it if I were you; after all your father wasn't around too much at the time.' Deanna confirms that her parentage was never in any doubt but admits that, even as a young girl 'I did get the drift!' It was many months before her father finally returned after the war.

He had been marooned on the other side of the world in Australia, having served on a minesweeper. The logistics of moving service personnel back to Britain from all over the globe meant it took almost a year for him to make it back to the UK. In the meantime the Australian government found people work on farms or in factories, to keep them occupied, and her father worked on a farm near Brisbane. The farmer took quite a shine to him and offered him a permanent job, with the opportunity to build a house for his family. But her mother was having none of it, when he revealed his hopes and plans for a new life down under. On the day he did eventually return home to Corby, Deanna was almost five years old, and on hearing his eager knock at the front door she peered tentatively out of the window. 'Mummy, Mummy, there's a man at the door,' she said. Her mother, anticipating her husband's return threw open the door and ran into his arms. Turning to her daughter she explained, 'That's not a man Deanna, that's your Dad.'

Deanna admits that she was far more interested in the exotic goodies he had brought back in his kit bag, than she was in him. 'Such was the lot of we war babies,' she ponders, 'born into a hostile world of conflict, our cognitive years formed without the presence of a father figure, with only the shadowy recollection of a stranger spending a few hours of very infrequent shore leave.' A letter sent to Deanna's father by her paternal grandmother, Alice Jane Dixon, while he was still in Australia is dated 4 January 1946, and was returned to her home address stamped, 'Return to sender: Addressee discharged from H.M. Service.' Today the letter has a certain poignancy.

> Dear Jack,
>
> Just a line or two to let you know we are all right now that the New Year has entered upon us. I hope you got our Christmas cards all right. I told George [his brother] that I hope this time in another year, all being well, we shall all be able to celebrate Christmas and the New Year together. The children brought their toys down to show us what Father Christmas had brought them. Deanna was delighted to bring her dolls pram and her dolly, she said it's name was 'Apple-Green'. Do-do [Deanna's sister, aged six] had a desk and chair, and Jennifer [aged eight] had a two-wheeled bike, and several other things. They got on all right considering everything is so shocking dear. I expect you are looking forward now to coming home. The time will not seem so long now that the New Year has come in; we are looking forward to you coming, as it seems ages since you went. We are getting terrible weather, frost at present but up to yet no snow. I expect you have weather like an English summer's day in Australia.

Ron Green's father had been in Gibraltar before returning to his family in Norfolk, and Ron says that he will never forget the night of his return. Among the goodies he presented them with were boiled sweets, which were a bit sticky as they were not individually wrapped. Ron, slightly aggrieved, suggests that his sisters aged nine and seven seemed to have more than their fair share. His father therefore hid the tin, but that night, as 'no doubt Mum and Dad were making up for lost time,' he states, the children found it, consumed some more of the sweets and put the tin back on the marble washstand behind the bed, where they had found it. Later that night, Ron was woken by his sisters, who said they could hear

158   *Homecoming.*

a 'plonking noise'. Suddenly Ron heard the plonk too and the three of them yelled in terror. Their father entered the room and sat on the bed asking, 'What's up?'

'We keep hearing a plonking noise,' he was told. All of a sudden there it was again, coming from behind the bed. An investigation found that they had put the sweet tin back upside down, and the sticky sweets were dropping at intervals from the bottom. 'That'll learn you,' Dad laughed. Mr Green also brought some oranges and bananas home. Ron's mother decided to take some for his grandmother in Norwich, on the No. 12 bus from Wynmodham, but lost them on the way. 'Dad was furious,' says Ron. 'All the way from Gib. and you lose them on a nine mile bus ride.'

Rosa Bowler remembers when her own father came home to East Ilsley. Kathleen, her sister, had never seen their father as he was away in India, and after he was demobbed they did not know when he would arrive. One Sunday morning Rosa heard car doors banging and looking out of the bedroom window, she could see her father had returned. She was excited and ran down to meet him, but Kathleen was frightened, and hid behind the door before running back up the stairs again. Although it was a time of great happiness and joy for the family, Rosa remembers her father being very quiet and pensive following his homecoming.

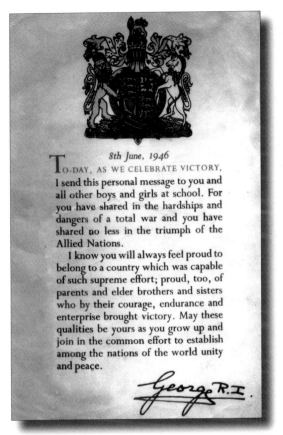

159 *Certificate sent to all school children after the war.*

8th June, 1946

TO-DAY, AS WE CELEBRATE VICTORY, I send this personal message to you and all other boys and girls at school. For you have shared in the hardships and dangers of a total war and you have shared no less in the triumph of the Allied Nations.

I know you will always feel proud to belong to a country which was capable of such supreme effort; proud, too, of parents and elder brothers and sisters who by their courage, endurance and enterprise brought victory. May these qualities be yours as you grow up and join in the common effort to establish among the nations of the world unity and peace.

George R.I.

When it was known a local soldier was returning there was often a big show of support from the community. At Ammanford in Wales, Myra Williams explains that every village would have a concert to raise money for a party in support of returning heroes. At Walford, Margaret Wilce states that their special party was for the homecoming of an uncle who had been a prisoner in Germany for a number of years. 'Along with my parents I went to welcome him home,' says Margaret. 'My aunt and grandparents had made a huge banner WELCOME HOME that they had hung across the front of the house. It was a terrible shock to see this skeleton-like man who before the war had been really round and cuddly. I was horrified when I held his hand, it was just bone and tight skin. He told us that his fellow prisoners were much worse than him as, not being a smoker, he had exchanged his cigarette ration for food.'

So what are the lasting impressions that those who were children have of this period in their lives? Marie Litchfield perhaps sums it up.

It never ceases to amaze me how people can continue to live normal lives in spite of the most abnormal and often terrible circumstances. There must be a built-in toughness in human nature that we don't reckon on when life is easier. The years of the war were not easy ones – to put it mildly – yet we all carried on, pulled together, sang a little song, and counted our blessings.

Tony King's final summing up is representative not only of where he lived in Portsmouth, but of London and all the other cities and major towns that suffered during the Blitz.

It is now many years since the last of the bombed buildings were demolished, and the city we can see today was built upon the ashes of the past. The air-raid shelters, the barrage balloons, and the static water tanks that stood at the street corner have now all vanished, along with most of the other stark reminders of those grim war years. The once grey and shadowy streets are ablaze with lights, and food is available aplenty in modern supermarkets. There are no more gaping craters to be avoided, no piles of filthy rubble to be stumbled over, no stinking pall of smoke hovering in a cloying smog of death and destruction, no more skeletons of once fine buildings reaching like gaunt fingers into the sky.

The gas masks have disappeared, along with ration books, national identity cards, posters urging us to 'dig for victory' and to 'save waste paper'. But even sadder for people of my generation, with the passing of the war the true British spirit of camaraderie that made everyone laugh at adversity has also passed into history. The automatic desire to pitch in to help everybody that was a part of life at that time has long since perished. 'Bombed out dear?' someone would say, 'Never mind, I'll make a nice cuppertee!' Down the road, the corner shop with its windows blown out by a near miss would boldly display the sign 'Business as usual'. The singsongs in the public shelters, the bawdy jokes about 'Old Adolf', the rationing, the sheer uncertainty of everything, maybe they were terrible times. But in a strange sort of way I felt safer then than I do now if I have to risk walking out in the city after dark!'

Index

References to illustrations are **bold**